AND
WHO
IS
MY
NEIGHBOR?

AND WHO IS MY NEIGHBOR?

*Poverty, Privilege,
and the Gospel of Christ*

Gerald W. Schlabach

HERALD PRESS
Scottdale, Pennsylvania
Waterloo, Ontario

Library of Congress Cataloging-in-Publication Data
Schlabach, Gerald.
    And who is my neighbor? : poverty, privilege, and the gospel
of Christ / Gerald W. Schlabach.
      p. cm.
    Includes bibliographical references.
    ISBN 0-8361-3525-3 (alk. paper)
    1. Church work with the poor. 2. Christianity and justice.
3. Church and social problems. 4. Love—Religious
aspects—Christianity. I. Title.
    BV639.P6S32 1990
    261.8'325—dc20   90-33713
                                                      CIP

The paper used in this publication meets the minimum requirements of
American National Standard for Information Sciences—Permanence of Paper
for Printed Library Materials, ANSI Z39.48-1984.

97 96 95 94 93 92 91 90 10 9 8 7 6 5 4 3 2 1

Contents

Foreword by John M. Perkins 7

Acknowledgments 9

Author's Preface 13

How to Use This Book for Group Study 17

Reading Our World, Reading the Bible

1. Blessed Are the Poor? 23

> *Poverty surely is not God's will. Yet somehow poverty is also a place to encounter God. How can this be?*

2. The Poor Are Us 34

> *The mad dash away from poverty has impoverished many Christians in new ways. For the church of the ex-poor, true wealth and security lie in rediscovering relationship to the poor.*

3. Christ, the Poor One 45

> *Reorienting personal and congregational lives toward the poor is a key to church renewal. Conversion to the poor is integral to conversion to Christ.*

4. When Did We See You? 58

> *While struggling for economic security, many have taken on values and attitudes that turn them away from the poor. They may even turn to the Bible for justification.*

5. Where Your Treasure Is,
There Will Your Heart Be 68

> *Poverty is not God's will for humanity. God offers us rich relationships with God, others, and creation. Valuing that true wealth transforms our priorities and life decisions.*

6. New Heavens, New Earth 79

> *God's kingdom is breaking into human history. We welcome signs of God's new ways here and now. God's purposes shape our visions as individuals, families, and congregations.*

7. Good News to the Poor 89

Will the gospel to the poor rob their dignity and hinder their initiative? Not if it is the freeing, enlightening, and empowering gospel that Jesus spoke of in Luke 4.

8. Learning to Read with the Poor 99

As the poor read the Bible together alongside needs, they discover a more active faith. The Bible will come alive for the nonpoor also as they strive to read it with them.

9. Who Is the Neighbor? 109

The good Samaritan models for us a life lived in solidarity with others. Conversion to the poor can happen as we recall the mercy and compassion God has shown to us.

10. What Shall We Do? 119

Work to alleviate poverty in local areas, yet make connections with global causes of poverty. Work together with the poor in outward-looking circles of faith and action.

11. A Closing Prayer 132

O Lord, to love you with all our heart, soul, mind, and strength, and to love our neighbors as ourselves are not burdensome commandments, but the grace and richness of life itself.

Making Connections

Introduction: To Know Christ, Obey Him 143

12. Poverty and Economic Injustice 148

13. Poverty, Militarism, and War 160

14. Poverty and Environmental Degradation 172

15. Cycles of Poverty and Webs of Culture 184

Arranging Encounters Between Middle- and Low-Income Groups 197

Questionnaire: Beginning Social Analysis 207

The Author 211

Foreword

AND WHO IS My Neighbor? is both relevant and timely. As I travel around the two-thirds world and observe difficulties related to poverty, I see more clearly the problems within North America. People are asking: What can I, just one person, do?

I believe that this book gives positive and concrete answers to that query, in a way that affirms the dignity of the poor. It calls for us to join ourselves with persons, listen to them, get to know them, learn from them, and also serve them.

We know that poverty exists, and as we see our own individual privileges and wealth, it's so easy for us to feel guilty about the situation. Here is a textbook that can be used by stalwart individuals, Sunday schools, and groups. It leads to definite action in making friendly connections.

This book allows the poor to tell their own story. We hear the groans, crying, and joy they experience. As we listen, we begin to understand what can be done to effect change.

Our welfare systems have not arisen from the cry and ache of the people affected. They come from researchers unrelated to the people. Many programs have created a great sense of dependence within the people who receive the funds. We call them welfare-dependent programs. Today much of our social action and counseling has become known as codependent: we help to perpetuate the problem that the person faces.

But Schlabach provides a road map which illustrates how we can first hear the people. By learning to listen, we will begin to trust them and walk alongside as we assist them, and we will be helped ourselves. We will help each other.

I think of people who work with the prison population of America and especially the black prison population. This book can become a manual for use as a counseling tool to rehabilitate those in jails.

Yes, we must affirm people's dignity, and not believe they have to be carbon copies of ourselves. We must allow others to be who they are based on their knowledge and experience. As we work locally, and begin to network nationally and internationally, we will begin to see all of humanity as our neighbor. We will become lovers of peace and begin to learn how to effectively coexist without war. We must believe that people can change, that they can come to know Jesus Christ and thereby be more joyful with what they have.

Most important, I believe we in the West, especially the United States, have to find ways we can live on less and enjoy it, then take what we save and use it in a way that people have defined for themselves. Yet we must understand that we may not change the total world condition within our lifetime.

And Who Is My Neighbor? provides crucial perspectives. I would like to see major Christian mission societies, and development and relief organizations, inviting their missionaries and interns to ponder the implications of this book. I believe it answers within its pages the question raised in its title.

Jesus himself said: "Thou shalt love the Lord thy God with all thy heart, . . . thy soul, . . . thy mind, and . . . thy strength: this is the first commandment. And the second is . . . this, Thou shalt love thy neighbour as thyself. There is none other commandment greater than these" (Mark 12:30-31, KJV). This book shows how we can get to know our neighbor, and sincerely begin to love our neighbor as we love ourselves.

John M. Perkins
Pasadena, California

Acknowledgments

SINCE 1920, Mennonite Central Committee (MCC) has been a foremost way that Mennonites and Brethren in Christ in North America have responded to human need on this continent and around the world. Through service in relief, development, peacemaking, and education for justice, MCC workers have seen hunger and poverty up close in many forms and places. They also have seen the wealth, wisdom, and faith of those who bear that ambiguous label "the poor."

In 1986, the Information Services staffs of Mennonite Central Committee in Akron, Pennsylvania, and Winnipeg, Manitoba, began planning an educational project on contemporary poverty, the Bible's perspective on poverty, and what the poor themselves might have to say about both. The MCC staff who conceived the project sought to pull together current information on poverty, perspectives gleaned from MCC workers, and extensive interviews with local people on each continent where MCC works. The hope was that the stories by the poor would communicate insights into poverty that facts and figures cannot.

Kristina Mast Burnett headed MCC Information Services throughout the period of gathering data and stories and writing. In 1987, while short-term staff member Randy Landis

Eigsti was collecting interviews, Mast Burnett asked me to organize and write a curriculum suitable for use in adult Sunday school classes, house fellowships, Bible studies, and congregational action groups concerned about poverty. I began this task the following year, after completing nearly five years of service in Nicaragua and Honduras. Mast Burnett's support, patience, and counsel were invaluable throughout the writing process.

Jocele and Art Meyer of the MCC U.S. Office of Global Education contributed to the project in many ways. Other MCC staff who read drafts and made suggestions include Renton Amell, Helen Glick, John Longhurst, Titus Peachy, Ardell Stauffer, and Cheryl Zehr Walker. Colleagues in Central America regularly expressed interest and encouragement. One of them, Mary Jane Newcomer, enriched this book greatly by sharing her own story.

Other readers were Marlene Kropf of the Mennonite Board of Congregational Ministries and Arnold Snyder of Conrad Grebel College, Waterloo. Gene Stoltzfus, Dorothy Friesen, and other members of Synapses, an action network for justice in Chicago, offered action ideas for "Making Connections."

Marvin Friedman Hamm's seminary thesis on conversion to the poor came to my attention at a fortuitous moment. His summary of trends that are deepening poverty, particularly in North America, helped me articulate my own emerging convictions and appear in the latter portions of chapter 2. He also allowed me to rework portions of that thesis for the appendix on "Arranging Encounters."

A number of years ago Fran Ringer urged me and other students in a class at Lancaster (Pennsylvania) Theological Seminary to use role-plays to study the Bible through the eyes of the poor. I have been grateful to him as I have elaborated on that method for the present study.

I am indebted to Ana D. Garcia and George S. Johnson for their list of face-to-face encounters from pages 12-13 of *Evangelism and the Poor,* copyright © 1986, The American Lutheran Church, and reprinted in chapter 3 by permission of Augsburg Fortress. The "Questionnaire: Beginning Social Analysis" is adapted from Joe Holland and Peter Henriot, S.J., *Social Analysis: Linking Faith and Justice*, revised and enlarged edition (Maryknoll, N.Y.: Orbis Books, 1980 and 1983), pages 106-109, and used with permission.

Special thanks go to those who provided interviews and case studies: Ron Byler, Lawrence Peters, John Morse, Rich Hostetler Meyer, Les Gustafson-Zook, Earl Martin, Luke Schrock-Hurst, Murray Nash, and Dale Nafziger. Mev Puleo, who traveled to Brazil as an intern with the Resource Center for Nonviolence in Santa Cruz, California, also shared from her many interviews with participants in Christian base communities in Brazil. In all, more than twenty people provided interviews that have enriched this project and our understanding of poverty. Unfortunately, only a few of the stories they collected could appear in this book.

Though many people have contributed, I have had to select and shape their suggestions and stories. I hope that I have succeeded in doing so with the respect and reverence that each one deserves. Above all, I hope that this book expresses my deep and permeating gratitude to many people who may never read this book. Those who opened their lives and shared their stories with my colleagues around the world surely belong among those who, like the apostle Paul, are "poor, yet making many rich" (2 Corinthians 6:10).

In these pages I mention Simón, Pedro, the co-op members of La Libertad, and Salvadoran refugees. I wish I could tell of many more Central Americans of different classes and faith communities who have enriched my faith through their stories. Then there are those who have guided me in my own imperfect efforts to develop new relationships with the poor and homeless here in North America. I think of Barbara, Vernon, and others at the Daytime Resource Center in Lansing, Michigan.

Finally, I must thank those who have walked with my family in our struggle to discover how God is calling us to faithfulness back in North America. In particular, members of the Michigan State University Mennonite Fellowship offered listening ears, counsel, extra child care, and a pilot study of these chapters.

John Rogers, as editor, belongs in this list of fellow pilgrims. In combining a trenchant pursuit of the clearest possible message with unfailing regard for my own story, he has helped create not just a manuscript but a friendship.

The colleague, friend, sister, and pilgrim who has contributed most is my wife. With joint hope that our sons Gabriel and Jacob will find a contagion of grace in the values and relationships celebrated here, I dedicate this book to my wife, Joetta.

Author's Preface

SIMÓN WAS FORTY-FIVE years old, a father of four, and a deacon in the church I was attending in San Pedro Sula, Honduras. He was also the poorest man in the congregation. All day he walked the streets selling toilet paper, toothpaste, and laundry soap. Most evenings he attended a special elementary school for adults. He wanted desperately to read, especially the Bible. He couldn't attend church as often as he liked. Not only did he study many evenings, but often he needed to sell seven days a week to survive.

Yet, in my memory, Simón was always at church. He greeted people at the door with a special warmth. He testified enthusiastically, witnessing to God's miracles in his life. He tithed his meager earnings more faithfully than any other member. And how he loved to pray!

One month I had a flu virus that simply refused to go away. After two weeks in bed, I was quite discouraged. The doctor shrugged his shoulders. My work piled up. My wife struggled to replenish her sympathy. I called on Simón.

I wish I could tell you that the day after Simón came over to pray for me, I got better. Simón, to be sure, was a man of faith. My own stores of energy, spiritual and otherwise, were pretty depleted by then. The bright spot, the ray of encouragement, that I recall from that dreary month in bed was Simón's face. I don't think Simón and his wife even had a separate bedroom in their tiny, disheveled house. But he entered mine with a wide smile, and he knelt to pray with intense focus.

Maybe I remember Simón so well because the light from his face showed me who I really was. I had a good doctor. I administered a $50,000 program for a relief-and-development agency. I had organizational backing. I had a college education, books on theology, poverty, and injustice. And I had a computer to put it all together. But I was on my back; and God's gift to me was Simón.

This is not just a book about poverty. It is first about people and their stories and only second about issues and their causes. It is first a call to relationship and then a call to action. It is about reading the Bible together with people like Simón.

This book also is not about how much poor people need what the nonpoor have to offer. Certainly many of us could be freer with our food for relief efforts, our money for development projects, our time for voluntary service, and our efforts for political change. But we need poor people at least as much as they need us.

As God used Simón to show me my poverty, poor people, who make up at least half the world's population, are a sign for all humanity. The Christ who says, "I was hungry . . . I was thirsty . . . I was naked . . . I was in prison, and you . . ." (Matthew 25:31-46, RSV)—this Christ is still among poor people. He speaks to us from there about our own lives and priorities. He reminds us that our choices may impoverish or enrich life—the lives of others and even our own.

Throughout the history of God's people, and in many parts of the world today, God has renewed the children of Abraham and reordered the church's priorities by putting the Bible in the hands of those whom society neglects, ignores, and exploits. Typically, they read it with fresh eyes.

Can we too learn to read the Bible with fresh eyes? Can we experience the gospel with a new excitement and challenge?

Can the gospel continue to free us from the molds that we cast for ourselves so that we might feel more secure?

Inviting poor people into our circles of church and community gives us one opportunity for such rediscovery. Their hard-won wisdom and insight are a gift to the church. Through them we may discover our own poverty and then gladly join Christ in circles of human relationship that are wide enough to include those whose poverty is more visible than ours may be.

As you work through this book, keep these goals before you:

● Look squarely and honestly at the things that impoverish our world, our society, and our own lives.

● Read the Bible *with* poor people by hearing their stories, putting yourselves in their shoes, and imagining what they might see as they read the Scriptures.

● Encounter poor people in your area directly, and begin to develop or deepen personal relationships with them.

● Prayerfully consider how to join together with others in your congregation or community to organize ongoing, active responses that aim at empowering poor people.

Love of God and love of neighbor are integrally linked. In Luke 10, Jesus made this clear. I hope that through this study you will be challenged and empowered to hear and live into Jesus' answer to the lawyer's question—a question that echoes throughout history: *And who is my neighbor?*

How to Use This Book for Group Study

THE BEST WAY to read this book is with others. If you are reading on your own, you should have no problem adapting and reflecting on most of the study questions for groups that close each chapter in the first part and that appear throughout the second part. But more is at stake than that.

One person *can* make a difference, but only if he or she joins with others in forging collective responses to human need. As you read on, you will find out why individualism only deepens human poverty. So even if you have picked up this book for personal reading, consider seeking out a friend or two to read it with you, discuss it, and plan for action.

The setting for group study may be a Sunday school class, a home Bible study, or an informal discussion group. Regardless, you can enhance your study together by incorporating the following approaches.

1. Take an extra week or two if necessary. If you study this book during a quarter in your church year, you will have thirteen weeks to cover eleven chapters. This will allow you to dedicate session time to one of the activities I propose. Or it will let you dedicate two sessions to a crucial section—like chapter 10, on planning how to respond. On the other hand, if you are part of a group that has considerably less than a full quarter for study, then focus on chapters 1, 2, 4, 6, 7, 9, and 10.

2. Learn to use role-play to study the Bible with the poor. Role-playing is a way to invite the poor into our circle of Bible study. Each week ask one or two people to imagine what the people who share their stories in these chapters would say if they were studying the Bible with you. Or the entire group might try to see through their eyes as you study.

Here are some steps to follow as you learn to put yourself in other people's shoes as you read the Bible. Even if you are reading this book on your own, or while you are reading in preparation for group study, you can use your imagination creatively to follow these steps:

• As you read the words of the poor, particularly in chapters 4 through 10, ask yourself these questions, and discuss them as a group the first few times:

—What are the most powerful forces shaping this person's life?

—What experiences are likely to be most prominent in his or her memory?

—Describe your "guest's" personality as you imagine it to be.

• Divide participants into smaller groups of three. In each group, at least one person should play the part of the guest. A second person might interpret the text in ways typical among people who are not poor, especially the first time you try role-playing. A third person should remain receptive to what both of the others have to say and ask them questions.

• Participants should be free to choose the roles they feel most comfortable playing, especially the first time. However, avoid close identification between the role being played and the person's real situation. Since the technique may be new to some, it may also seem threatening. Group leaders should encourage, but not pressure, participants to take the plunge. If some want only to play the observer role, allow that, even if this requires reshuffling units.

● Study the text and answer discussion questions, all the while retaining assigned roles.

● When the entire group gathers together again, always debrief. Ideally, every group, and every person in each group, should have a chance to tell how they felt in their respective roles or what they saw as observers. If the class is large and time only permits general discussion, at least make sure that responses come from some people in all of the roles.

—Was it hard to play the role of the guest? Why or why not?

—Was it hard to find an interpretation of the text that was typical of those who are not poor? Why or why not?

—What did the role-players do that observers found especially helpful? How would they suggest that people portray someone like your guest next time?

● What new insights did you gain about the text of Scripture that you studied? Summarize the responses to any study questions.

3. Begin developing personal relationships with the poor. In early chapters I will urge you to plan for face-to-face encounters with poor people. The sooner you start exploring possibilities in your local area, the better. Specific ideas for personal encounter accompany chapter 3. You will also find guidance in an appendix on "Arranging Encounters Between Middle- and Low-Income Groups." Reading it will help you approach poor people with sensitivity and respect even if you are not part of a group encounter.

If you have hesitations about these ideas at first, that's fine. You may have a different perspective as you get farther into these studies. All I ask is that you remain open to finding new ways to learn to know the poor as people.

By the time you study chapter 6, you may find new ways to meet poor people in your local area. If so, you will be in a better position to follow that chapter's directions for making an initial assessment of the needs and efforts to alleviate poverty in your local area. The appended "Questionnaire: Beginning Social Analysis" will be a useful tool. If you find new ways to meet poor people by the time you study chapter 10, you will be in a better position to plan an active response.

4. Incorporate worship experiences throughout. Learning is a matter not just of the mind but also of the heart. At the end of each chapter are suggestions for personal meditation labeled "Learning by Heart". The primary focus is the good Samaritan story. Be sure to give yourself time to work with these. Another way to incorporate worship—and to tie your study into the life of your congregation even more—is to use chapter 11 as a resource for planning a worship service in which your group shares its learning and responses with others.

5. Expect to act in response to the poor. You would not have bought this book without some faith that change is possible in our world. You would not invest time and energy in this study process without some hope for change. So, as you look towards the final chapters of the first part of the book, you will want to be open to the possibility that they will not be final at all. Growing commitment to people who are poor, and direct involvement in their lives, may lead you or your group to continue the process of learning and acting.

"Making Connections," the second part of the book, provides resources to help you and your group form an ongoing response to poor people. Through prayer, reflection, and study you can find a way that fits your local situation and your specific concerns about global needs. The introduction to part 2, "To Know Christ, Obey Him," suggests different ways to use these resources.

Reading Our World, Reading the Bible

1
Blessed Are the Poor?

Have you ever been hungry for more than twenty-four hours? Have you ever given up meals so your children could eat? Have your children ever been sick for an unusually long time and you couldn't afford to take them to a doctor?

Have you ever envied someone for enjoying things so basic as food, clean water, and shelter? Have you ever had to pretend not to hear your child's request for a simple treat? Have you ever felt bitter at the whole world?

Have you ever been so in debt that you could hardly imagine getting out, yet needed to go even farther into debt to try? Have you ever been evicted from your home or farm? Have you ever sought work for more than three months, while the bills piled up? Have you ever been uprooted from your home or family against your will?

If you answered yes to any of these questions, then you know what it means to be poor. You know the power of poverty to warp the shape and wound the texture of life itself. Even if you couldn't answer yes to any of these questions, experiences of poverty probably have shaped you in some way. All our forebears were refugees, immigrants, or slaves. All probably experienced some degree of poverty. Some experienced economic exploitation and oppression.

Who among us has *never* felt the inside of human poverty? Who has *never* felt powerless? Without hope, direction, or vision? Listless and without energy to confront some current challenge? A victim of forces or circumstances beyond our control? Unsure of how we would get through another week, or even a day? Who has never perceived that people and situations were bringing out the worst in us, yet we were too desperate to care?

The poverty that most of us usually recall is crisis—times that put us to the test and perhaps drew us closer to God. But what if we stretched those crises into lifetimes? If you can imagine this, then you can begin to understand what it means to live your whole life in poverty—as more than two billion of the world's people do. Unlike our own, the poverty of the world's two billion poor—many of whom are children—is too broad, too deep, and too immediate for them to live a single day without knocking up against it. Theirs is a poverty that boggles the mind:

—100,000,000 people have no shelter whatsoever.
—770,000,000 do not get enough food for an active
                working life.
—500,000,000 suffer from iron-deficiency anemia.
—1,300,000,000 do not have safe water to drink.
—800,000,000 live in "absolute poverty," unable
                to meet minimal demands.
—880,000,000 adults cannot read and write.
—10,000,000 babies are born malnourished every year.
—14,000,000 children die of hunger-related causes every
                year.[1]

Our experiences of poverty may be relatively small in comparison. Still our suffering, our poverty, can become a bond between those who carry the name "poor" and those who do not. Sensing a shared human poverty calls forth empathy. We feel the suffering of others as our own. A growing empathy motivates solidarity. We stand with others in their suffering. Solidarity prompts acts that bind us together even more. We work together to alleviate suffering.

God calls all of us to recognize our poverty. God offers it as a place to encounter ourselves as we truly are. In turn, we face our need for God and others. Such awareness may be hardest for those of us whom the world does not call "poor." We do not have constant, gnawing, material reminders of our need. Apparent abundance fills our lives with plush illusions to the contrary. Society tells us lies, that we need what we do not need, that we already have what we need most!

When we do break through these illusions to see ourselves as we really are, we can finally sense God's abiding love for what it really is. This is a moment of grace and glory. Embracing our own poverty is the path to life, to God, to others.

But then comes the temptation to think of our *spiritual poverty* as if it were the only kind that matters. When we regard spiritual poverty in a way that makes the grinding poverty of two billion lifetimes seem smaller, trivial, or less important than our own, we backslide. We slide back into self-deception. We fail to see ourselves for who we are in this world. We invite complacency. And we only impoverish our spirits more!

Someone has said, "There is a link between meaningless lives in the first world and meaningless deaths in the third world." But there is a way to inject our lives with new meaning—and perhaps shrink the size of our own problems as we mature. That way is to become more intimately involved in what is on God's heart: the poverty of the two billion and the unjust, meaningless deaths among them.

"We have been trained to believe that fulfillment comes to those who make their lives an endless round of partygoing with plenty of laughs," says Tony Campolo. But "Jesus tells us that people who cry because their hearts are broken over the things that break the heart of God are the fulfilled people in this world."[2]

Poverty Defined

Governments, banks, and development agencies have official definitions of poverty. Inevitably, they define according to what they can measure—usually money and food. But official definitions can't measure the insides of poverty. So they tempt us to dehumanize poor people even more. If we describe poverty only in terms of money and food, we are likely to think of the solutions solely in terms of money and food. Obviously, both are extremely important. But a prisoner on death row can have money tucked away and an ample diet; yet he has no future, no freedom, little dignity, no options. The same holds true for those whom poverty imprisons.

Peter Townsend defines poverty as "the lack of resources necessary to permit participation in activities, customs, and diets commonly approved by society."[3] This is better. As long as poverty does not eat away at life itself, those who appear poor economically may remain rich in ways that our impersonal and individualistic societies have nearly forgotten. It is when the bonds that hold people together begin to give way that poor people are impoverished indeed.

An African elder in the nomadic Wodaabe tribe tells of a year of great drought. The herds of cattle that sustain the nomadic way of life died. Clans dispersed to villages. There they begged and lived in unaccustomed ways to survive. "No more mutual help. No more friendship. Each man thought only of his stomach. Yes, for us it was even worse than death."[4]

Speaking from a different setting—a Chicago housing development—Valerie Werner, a single parent of three, agrees. "I define poverty as lack of security and being extremely vulnerable. Your basic needs aren't being met; and the only one that you can really depend on to have those needs met is yourself because you are not in a community that is working together to meet each others' needs. The poorer you get in this country and the further away from any kind of community support or people support, the harder it is to get out of it."

When material needs go unmet, poor people lose one simple choice after another. Eventually the future itself closes. A teacher of the deaf in Brazil explains that being poor in Brazil "means a person doesn't have financial means that are sufficient to have a dignified life, doesn't have financial abilities to get a good education, to get a good high school education, to buy books and materials needed." Without money for good nutrition, the body suffers. Without money for wholesome recreation, the mind and spirit suffer.

Often a wife will suffer most. "She has to do with the money that comes in, and always the money coming in buys less and less." The president and others in power are to blame, says the teacher; "but very subtly the guilt is passed on to the poor people. So persons will try to escape through other methods such as drinking and things like that."

F. Kefa Sempangi, director of the Africa Foundation, a Christian relief-and-development organization, is more blunt. Poverty "is not a lack of things; it is not having only one television or one car. Our poverty is a demonic force which enters human life and threatens to destroy it completely. It causes men and women, boys and girls, to be so ground into the dirt that their spirits are destroyed. It breaks all social norms, down to the smallest rule of hygiene. Human life itself becomes the cheapest commodity."

Poverty is anti-life, death. All that makes people human, all that expresses the image of God, begins dying long before the body dies. Elie Wiesel tells of the particularly demonic form of human deprivation that the Nazis inflicted on their victims in German concentration camps. But the power of hunger as he describes it respects no barbed-wire confines:

"Hunger means humiliation. A hungry person experiences an overwhelming shame. All desires, aspirations, and dreams lose their lofty qualities and relate to food alone. It fills one's universe. Diminished by hunger, one's spirit is diminished as well. One's fantasy wanders in quest of bread. One's prayer rises not toward God but toward a bowl of milk."

A Bolivian peasant expresses this diminished human existence another way: "The hoe, and the hoe, and the hoe is all we know. And if you aren't good and tough, the hoe will kill you. That's right, you don't last long unless you are really hard and tough."

As poverty steals hope itself, poor people may accept destitution as their fate. "You can't change it," they say. "It's God's will." Those with power have always said inequity and exploitation were part of the natural order. Those with secular power call this "survival of the fittest." Those with religious power call it "God-ordained." Eventually, poor people come to agree. "The dynamics of being poor are such that the oppressed poor finally accept the inhumanity and humiliation of their situation; they accept the status quo as the normal course of life. Thus, to be poor becomes both a state of things and an attitude to life, an outlook, even a worldview."[5]

And in a South American slum, a poor grandmother sits rocking. She is looking into the eyes of the unwanted child of her unmarried daughter. Absentmindedly she murmurs: "You're going to die, you're going to die, you're going to die."

What Blessing, Jesus?

Poverty is hardly God's will. Poverty is anti-life. It is demeaning. It is death. Yet God works in a special way *among* poor people, *for* poor people, and *through* poor people. We see it throughout the pages of history. We see it wherever thoroughgoing church renewal takes place. We see it throughout the pages of the Bible. And we see it throughout our world today, if we look.

What shall we make of this? If poverty is not God's will, how can it be such a pivotal place for meeting God and knowing God's will? Jesus stated our problem early in his ministry: "Blessed are the poor."

There are two versions of the Beatitudes, one in Matthew and one in Luke. But that is not our problem. Even the *easy* version is hard. Christians have argued over which version to put at the center of Jesus' teachings about the poor. Matthew 5:3-6 has it this way:

> Blessed are the poor in spirit,
>   for theirs is the kingdom of heaven.
> Blessed are those who mourn,
>   for they will be comforted.

> Blessed are the meek,
>> for they will inherit the earth.
> Blessed are those who hunger and thirst
>> for righteousness [justice],
>> for they will be filled.

The *poor in spirit* are brokenhearted and humble in spirit (Isaiah 61:1), aware of the poverty of human resources, and looking to God for care. They are in bodily misery—a basic meaning often overlooked by readers of Matthew—yet are blessed and possess the kingdom because they "know their need of God" (NEB).

Luke 6:20-26 is more concrete. Jesus presents contrasting fates of rich and poor. This leaves no doubt about the kind of poverty Jesus had in mind, according to Luke.

> Blessed are you who are poor,
>> for yours is the kingdom of God.
> Blessed are you who hunger now,
>> for you will be satisfied.
> Blessed are you who weep now,
>> for you will laugh. . . .
> But woe to you who are rich,
>> for you have already received your comfort.
> Woe to you who are well fed now,
>> for you will go hungry.
> Woe to you who laugh now,
>> for you will mourn and weep. . . .

"What kind of poverty is [Jesus] talking about? If you have a lot of money, you'll probably say spiritual poverty. If you have little or no money, you'll probably say physical poverty. The rich will thank God for Matthew; the poor will thank God for Luke."[6]

But why argue over something nobody really wants? Normal folks don't welcome either material or spiritual poverty. If liking either state came naturally—if we really *felt* blessed—we would want more. The so-called spiritually poor would want to be economically poor too. Why miss out on even greater blessing? The argument would be over! But this is definitely not our idea of happiness.

Let's think again of the poverty that the nonpoor experience, even if only in times of crisis. A wealthy corporate executive watches his wife struggling in intensive care following an auto accident. A young woman, midway through college, begins to overcome depression. Amid lapses of low self-esteem, she wonders whether God might love her after all. A two-career couple learns that their teenager is on drugs. Almost too late, they realize they have given him everything but their time.

Each of these people faces a deeply tragic situation. But each faces an opportunity as well. Nothing is automatic. Clarity may result, or bitterness. Each one has the opportunity to set new priorities. Each has a chance to reject false goals for life. There is a chance to admit one's need for God and to put people first again. In a special way, God is present. There is renewed love for the victim of neglect. And if the person herself is the victim, that may mean a new, healthy self-love and self-respect.

So too in the life of all humanity. Shouldn't we expect God to be most passionately involved precisely where need is greatest? "We should not be surprised that, in his universal love, God chooses to be a God of and for the poor," writes Ana de Garcia. God's special love, even partiality, for poor people, "does not contradict the fact that God is love and that he desires the wholeness and salvation of all people, rich and poor alike. God loves everybody, but not in any which way." God's love reaches out to all with the good news of the kingdom. The world's downtrodden challenge us that the only way to enter this kingdom is through Jesus' call to follow him through "repentance, justice, and love."[7]

What of the nonpoor? Garcia welcomes the question. "God's special love for the poor, rather than discriminating against the nonpoor, is a guideline for their priorities and behavior. . . . 'Blessed are the poor' points to the values around which we should organize our lives and the struggle to which we should put our energy."[8]

From Tragedy to Opportunity

World poverty is tragedy and neglect writ large across human history. It is no more God's will than a loved one's auto accident, a recurring depression, or a neglected teenager's drug abuse. Most victims of poverty have suffered, not from accidents, but from the choices others make, the neglect others condone, the injustices others commit in the name of getting ahead. Yet it too is an opportunity to look hard at our choices, our values, our priorities.

The world's poor are a message to church, to society, to those responsible for oppression—to all humanity: *Favor what God favors, the victims, the neglected, justice, and life itself. It is our opportunity.*

God will show love to people who are poor, and they will act upon it, with or without us. "Good news to the poor" offers them much more than a way to bear their burdens patiently. Just as it does for the young woman fighting depression, God's love offers poor people renewed dignity and self-esteem. With these, they begin to reclaim the gifts of land and community, health and know-how, that their oppressors have stolen from them.

Their good news can be our good news. We must choose. Even though God loves all—poor and nonpoor—there is one fateful difference. Poor people do not need privileged people to respond to God's love. But when privileged people try to respond to God yet continue to ignore people who are poor, they deceive themselves and only deepen their spiritual poverty.

"Feasting on the bounty of the earth is not our sin," writes Ken Sehested. "The pitfall comes as we eat in isolation from the needs of the poor. It simply is not possible to love God while we neglect the suffering of our neighbors."[9]

• • •

Learning by Heart

Read Luke 10:25-37; then reread verse 30.
This chapter invites you to recall experiences of poverty

that have helped shape your life. As you sit quietly, think back to some of these. If any one memory stands out as particularly painful or enduring, dwell with it for a while. Remember the feelings that you had while in that situation. Are there ways that you identify with the one who fell into the hands of robbers on the Jerusalem-Jericho road, who was stripped and beaten and left half dead?

Having recalled the experiences of poverty that belong to you, your friends, or your family, now recall the poverty of the two billion—stripped of resources and often of dignity, beaten down by both animosity and indifference, and left alone to die alone. Go back to the statistics on the scope of world poverty at the beginning of this chapter (page 24). When you read such facts, or encounter similar ones on the news, how do you feel: angry, despairing, numbed, apathetic, defensive, something else? Who do you want to blame: God, *the system,* yourself, the source of information?

• • •

For Thought and Discussion

1. What do you think Jesus meant when he said the poor are blessed? Reread the Beatitudes as they appear in Matthew 5:3-10 and Luke 6:20-26. Does "blessed are the poor" mean God wills that poor people remain in their poverty? Do you believe God shows special love and favor to people who are poor? Explain.

2. Do you find it helpful to speak of *spiritual poverty* in contrast to material or economic poverty? Does such language help you identify with the world's poor people? Do you sense any danger in speaking of poverty in these ways?

3. Someone has said, "There is a link between meaningless lives in the first world and meaningless deaths in the third world." How would you describe this link? What other, more lifegiving, bonds could link you to the world's poor and replace the link you have just described? How might you celebrate and strengthen that bond?

Notes

1. Ruth Leger Sivard, *World Military and Social Expenditures, 1987-88* (Washington, D.C.: World Priorities, 1987), p. 25.

2. Tony Campolo, commenting on Jesus' second beatitude, in foreword to Tom Sine, *Why Settle for More and Miss the Best? Linking Your Life to the Purposes of God* (Waco, Tex.: Word Books, 1987), p. xi.

3. Quoted in Ana de Garcia and George S. Johnson, *Evangelism and the Poor: A Biblical Challenge for the Church* (Minneapolis: American Lutheran Church, 1986), pp. 14-15.

4. Angelo Malike, *Beldum: Joy and Suffering Among the Wodaabe,* translated by Cordeen Gorder (Jos, Nigeria: JCMWA/MICCAO Assemblée, 1984), pp. 20-21.

5. The Reverend Canaan Banana, President of Zimbabwe, to the World Conference on Mission and Evangelism in Melbourne, Australia, in 1980.

6. Clarence Jordan, *The Sermon on the Mount,* rev. ed. (Valley Forge, Pa.: Judson Press, 1952, 1970), p. 20.

7. De Garcia and Johnson, p. 8.

8. De Garcia and Johnson, p. 15.

9. Ken Sehested, "Who (in Heaven's Name) Cares?" *Seeds,* August 1981.

2

The Poor Are Us

JOHN WESLEY KNEW as much about good news to poor people as any man in his generation. But he was worried. Looking into the poverty of his own heart, Wesley had shuddered. "How can I preach when I have not faith myself?" Looking at the poverty in the streets and offices of his own nation, he had wept. The England of Wesley's day was the most powerful nation on earth. Yet millions lived in squalor and worked in dangerous, demeaning factories.

Looking at the impoverished soul of the church he loved, Wesley was appalled. While prelates lived opulent lives, the Church of England neglected its dispirited working-class flocks in the nation's new industrial towns. And looking deeply as he did—not turning away from the poverty in himself, his nation, and his church—Wesley had met God.

As Wesley shared the fire that burned in his heart, he had seen God spark a mighty renewal. It was not the kind he had expected. He had hoped to renew the Church of England he loved and rescue it from its wealthy, cultured complacency. But it had turned him out of its pulpits and scoffed at his preaching. So he took his message into the streets. And poor people heard him gladly.

Good news for the poor meant more than street preaching,

however. The new converts needed care and training in the Christian life. Throughout his life, Wesley sought to avoid founding a competing church. Yet a new kind of church did emerge. It was in many ways more original than the later Methodist denomination. It was more radical and democratic than Wesley himself.

Wesley ordained lay pastors to follow up his evangelistic efforts. The lay leaders organized thousands of *clubs, bands, societies,* and *classes.* These were circles where working-class folks could feel at home. No unwritten codes of membership here. No need for fancy clothes, King's English, and other outward signs of respectability. The new converts gathered for prayer, Bible study, and training in living the Christian life. And the changes kept coming.

Soon these Christians brought good news to other poor people in different ways. Wesley insisted that his societies distribute clothing and food to the needy. He set a personal example by giving and raising funds.

Projects to aid the sick sprang up. The movement spawned a lending bank, offices to provide legal advice, housing for widows and orphans. One meeting hall in London created jobs by doubling as a workshop for milling and spinning cotton. Sunday schools taught practical skills as well as the Bible.

Historians note that "the Revival encouraged a passion for social justice."[1] Wesley himself, and other Methodists, took a keen interest in prison reform. In the next century, trade-union leaders emerged in disproportionate numbers from the Methodist ranks. Above all, followers of Wesley took seriously his own condemnation of slavery. They led campaigns to banish slavery in British colonies, as well as British participation in the slave trade.

"The Evangelical Revival made England aware of its social obligations."[2] Wesley put it this way: "The Gospel of Christ knows no religion but social, no holiness but social holiness. This command have we from Christ, that he who loves God love his brother also."[3]

Wesley, then, had witnessed a mighty revival. Yet he still confessed to a fear. "I do not see how it is possible, in the nature of things, for any renewal of true religion to continue long." His experience showed all too clearly that "wherever riches have increased, the essence of religion has decreased in the same proportion." What would happen as new Christians rebuilt their lives? "Industry and frugality" would follow, "and these cannot but produce riches. But as riches increase, so will pride, anger and the love of the world in all its branches."[4]

Caught in the Middle

When forced to choose between a powerful, worldly-wise church of the rich and a marginal-yet-vibrant church of the poor, Wesley's decision was relatively simple. He chose the streets, not the cathedrals. But as Wesley's life and ministry drew to a close, he felt caught. Behind him stood the church that had first said yes to the message of Jesus Christ, yes to good news to the poor. Before him loomed the church he knew was coming—the church of the ex-poor.

How would they keep the fire burning? How could they preserve trust in true riches—the wealth of faith, works, and fellowship they had once known? How would they replenish and reinvest that rich heritage of faith, so that God's kingdom might come near and God's "will be done on earth as it is in heaven"? Oh, how I wish that Wesley had told us! For we are the church that Wesley feared! Many of us belong to the church of the ex-poor.

"Wait a minute," you may say. "I'm not a Methodist!" Well, I'm not either. But the pattern Wesley foresaw is common to many Christian traditions. In North America especially, most churches began as immigrant churches, on the frontier, churches of dirt farmers and factory workers. Some had fled religious persecution in Europe. Others had fled poverty.

We, our parents, or our grandparents have striven mightily to put poverty behind us. Many have succeeded. But we haven't stopped at a comfortable lifestyle. We strive on. In the process, we draw farther and farther back from the face of the poor at home and abroad. After all, they represent everything we are trying to escape. They remind us what we could become if the bottom falls out. No empire lasts forever, and we know we can always slip into poverty again. The insurance industry is a monument to that insecurity.

We were right to have fled Egypt. But I worry that we are fleeing the wilderness too. Egypt was the place of slavery, oppression, harsh demeaning labor, and powerless vulnerability. These things were not God's will for Abraham's children, the industrial workers of Wesley's England, or our own children. Yet it was on the way out of Egypt, while still in the barren wilderness, that we encountered our God. In the wilderness, our needs and poverty were obvious, but so was God's glorious purpose for our lives. Unfortunately, God's people rarely flee Egypt without soon abandoning the lessons of the wilderness (see Deuteronomy 6:10-12; 8:1-20).

Church Among the Poor: God's Gift

Last year my family returned to the United States after five years of service in Central America. We had taken part in a wide range of activities, from emergency relief efforts to theological education. In many forms, ways, and settings we encountered the church among poor people. They certainly had their struggles and differences, but within their earthen vessels was a treasure. The faith and humble wisdom of Simón, whose story I told earlier, was one such treasure. I also remember La Libertad.

In 1981 five hundred families took over idle land on a huge plantation near La Libertad, Santa Bárbara. In Honduras, despite a history of military dictatorships, the law books agree that idle or underused land should go to those who will make it produce. Still, claiming the land is hardly easy. Government red tape is endless. Wealthy landowners have friends in high places. When the process bogs down, the only way the peasants can jar it loose is to move onto the land, set up their shanties, and start planting. If they are numerous and persistent enough to stand firm, the government may finally recognize their claim.

Such a stand takes more than desperation. It takes commitment and persistence. Commitment takes time. And persistence takes faith. Before the peasant families could act to recover the land, community leaders spent three years talking to families, organizing, talking together about the causes of their poverty, investigating their legal rights, and planning. It has taken faith in God and in one another to stick together since.

For the cooperatives around La Libertad, reading the Bible and seeking God's will is central to their life together. Ordinary business meetings begin with reading a passage of Scripture and discussing what it means in their setting. Classes in basic hygiene and health care, agriculture, or even bookkeeping often draw on examples from the Bible. Members include both Roman Catholics and Protestant Evangelicals.

The people of La Libertad are being the people of God. "We are still poor. We still have a lot of needs," one peasant told me. "But we have left the slavery we were under, looking for a day's work here, a week's work there, collecting firewood to sell." Said another woman, "We have had a change of life. Before we were in a state of ignorance and couldn't see or speak with outside people because we were ashamed. But we see how all this has changed."

The people of La Libertad, Santa Bárbara, are a sign of God's kingdom. They are a witness of hope. Their example speaks to us: "Don't put spiritual needs in one box, and material needs in another. Don't build your churches in the sky. Be God's people here on the earth, here on the land we work and share. Come, read the Bible with us, here in this school we built ourselves. Then go home and help us. Your government sends arms to our government, which jails us when we claim our rights. We need clean water, clinics, land reform, and agricultural aid. We don't need more soldiers. Please, we are grateful for the goats and technical help you give so that we can help ourselves. But be our voice in your country as well."

It is a message I have heard over and over again throughout Central America. "We can't leave," a Salvadoran woman in a refugee camp once told my wife and me. "So you must take our message. You are participants in our voice." Her words were like a sacred commission.

In Simón, God's gift was to show me who I am. In peasants and refugees like these, God's gift was to show me who I could be—a participant in the coming of a kingdom that is already "good news to the poor." But the refugee woman's words are also part of the reason I now live in North America. They have thrust me back into Wesley's dilemma, caught between the church among the poor and the church among the ex-poor.

Church Among the Ex-Poor: Our Dilemma

Recently a middle-class congregation near a Midwest city installed two of my friends as pastoral couple. The worship service was a true celebration for guests and congregation alike. My friends are the right people, in the right place, at the right time, with wisdom beyond their years. They have a clear vision of God's salvation drama at work down through the ages. They care deeply about social justice. Their style is to nurture, enable, and "prepare God's people for works of service" (Ephesians 4:12).

The congregation has much to offer to the work of God's kingdom. They are a gifted bunch. The professions they have chosen provide valuable community services. There are teachers, health care professionals, social workers. One prominent businessman in the congregation is active in a Christian organization that builds low-cost housing for people who are homeless. His business donates its services to that effort, and he is not too sophisticated to give his own time pounding nails. But something troubled me as one of my friends spoke during their installation service.

"Our denomination is increasingly urban," she said, mentioning congregations where she had served, and predicting that many things would be similar in this new one. "I already hear people saying the same things I have heard elsewhere: 'We are a diverse group. We often live far apart and drive many miles to meet together. And we are very, very busy.'

Our challenge is to be the church amid our diversity, distance, and busyness."

Diversity is good. It was a part of God's original creation, which God called good. And diversity will be part of creation's fulfillment when from "every tribe and language and people and nation" we sing Christ's praises (Revelation 5:9-14). In fact, the congregation, for all its exciting variety of gifts, could have used a little more diversity. All the cars in the parking lot looked like they would make it to another Sunday morning. Nearly everyone's skin was the same color. Being an urban congregation obviously didn't mean certain neighborhoods. I wondered if distance and busyness were among the reasons.

Distance and busyness—is this the life we have made for ourselves now that we've made it? Is this the wealth we have worked so hard to create? Must we simply accept these as givens, the narrow confines within which we must squeeze some place for the gospel?

Distance and busyness—I felt caught again. Does the gospel have nothing to say about these realities? Has it no power to transform them? Or will distance and busyness transform me and my family first? Will they keep us from new friends in the church among the poor, which is often hidden in North America?

Made It!—Made What?

Tom Sine, a Christian *futurist*, notes that many Christians, like others in our society, are trying to "make it to the top" without having any idea what they will find when they get there. As he begins his book *Why Settle for More and Miss the Best?* he tells a story of immense loneliness and distance from any kind of community.[5]

It is the story of a retired couple, Mr. and Mrs. Rose, who "live in a huge mansion on a two-hundred-acre estate" in Massachusetts. Having spent their lives amassing a multimillion-dollar fortune, they now live out their lives in a lonely vigil protecting it. "Their estate is ringed with security devices. But they constantly worry that rats will eat through the electrical system, leaving them unprotected. So, they have hired a Canadian couple to augment their security systems and to watch their house, particularly when they are gone. And then they have people come by periodically and drop in on the couple they hired to check up on them. They trust no one, and live with chronic fear."

Their elaborate security measures failed to protect them when their only son was murdered. "And they discovered in the midst of this crisis that they had so distanced themselves from other people that they had no one to turn to—not even each other." Mrs. Rose now sits for hours in her sitting room, rocking. She is alone, except for an old hound that sits on her lap.

Mrs. Rose's obsession with security taunts most of us from some shadowy corner of our minds. It is a picture of living out our last years alone, abandoned, without friends or kin, renting a dreary room with a meager social security check, perhaps even homeless. It is a picture of dying poor in every way. But except for the cash flow and the room, it is precisely the world that Mrs. Rose has made for herself by "making it."

The case is extreme. Those of us who are neither rich nor poor—but simply the nonpoor, the relatively privileged—may never expect to be in either Mrs. Rose's sitting room or homeless and on the street. Yet distance and busyness are constantly gnawing away at the quality of our lives, right in the suburbs where we have moved to "get away from it all"—an *all* that includes many urban poor people. But it can easily include our next-door neighbors as well.

Mrs. Rose reminds us just how close to home lie the sources of poverty—in our own individualistic ways, our choice to live for and to ourselves. In fact, Mrs. Rose illustrates three trends that are impoverishing many other lives as well. Sitting in her mansion, as alone as any bag lady, Mrs. Rose portrays *the breakdown of community.*

An overall trend toward the *centralization of economic and political power* in society has made it possible for her to amass her financial resources. And thanks to the tenets of *individual-*

ism, she honestly believes she is wealthy. Long ago this belief system convinced her that anyone with money and power would be able to secure a happy life regardless of what happens to others.

These trends and this poverty are subtle. Not all of us suffer them to the same degree. Yet the trends that have made our middle-class worlds have already unmade some other people's lives. They are the ones we usually think of as poor.

The *breakdown of community* has segregated many poor people into inner-city neighborhoods and forgotten mountain hollers. They are no longer our neighbors, as they were in small towns. Those small towns had their racial segregation and their "other side of the tracks" too. But face-to-face relationships often cushioned the effects of poverty.

There was a place in the town's lore and hearts for the town drunk. There was a job in the park for the man who had always been a little slow. There were visits to the elderly. Now our society pays professional caregivers, like social workers and welfare administrators, to do the work for us— sort of. With poor people "out of sight and out of mind," we find it easier and easier to cut their funding.

Centralization of power leaves poor people little control over their own lives. They live at the margins of economic and political life. A factory closes on short notice and moves overseas in search of cheap labor. The community that gave its sweat and blood for two generations reels in disbelief and starts to disintegrate. The workers overseas dare not organize unions or protest for better wages because others will gladly take their jobs. They have little say in the decisions their governments make.

Meanwhile, thanks to the tenets of *individualism,* those who do have power sleep soundly, without pangs of conscience. If they can make it, so can others. So poverty must be the fault of poor people themselves. Anyway, wealth will trickle down to the poor eventually. After all, an "invisible hand" guides the economy, transforming decisions motivated by personal greed into the common good. If some people fall through the cracks, individual charity can take care of them. So the argument goes. . . , while poor people wait for the trickle and hang through the cracks by their fingernails.

Poor people, then, are a sign of who we are rapidly becoming whenever we choose to avoid them in our mad scramble to make it. In a real way, when we meet people who are poor, we discover that they are us.

Is there hope? John Wesley nearly despaired, for the church he knew was moving too hard and fast in a direction away from poor people. But I think there is an answer to Wesley's question. Today many Christians who are among the privileged are experiencing renewal and finding hope as they recover relationships with people who are poor.

● ● ●

Learning by Heart

Read Luke 10:25-37; then reread verse 32.

In a sense, the priest and Levite in Jesus' story were victims too. They were trapped in a religious system that numbed their hearts even as it overwhelmed them with obligations. The Levites were the ones who cleaned the temple and all its vessels, the ones who led the singing and counted the money. They were indispensable. In fact, the Levites were a lot like many conscientious, harried, and overworked lay people who hold many congregations together today.

Do you ever feel so obligated to do many "good" things that you can't do the best and most important? Do your commitments sometimes make it necessary for you to "pass by on the other side," trying not to notice the one who has been stripped and beaten and left half dead?

Spend some time thinking about an occasion when you were the priest or the Levite. What were you thinking and feeling as you "passed by on the other side"?

Then think about a time when a "priest" or "Levite" passed by on the other side and left you stripped and beaten and half dead. What were you thinking and feeling as he or she tried to ignore you or hoped that you wouldn't notice them or call out for help?

• • •

For Thought and Discussion

1. What do you know about your congregation's or your denomination's previous experiences of poverty or suffering? How has affluence changed its priorities, sense of renewal, experience of God? What has it lost? What has it gained?

2. Read Deuteronomy 8:7-20. Imagine that John Wesley were going to preach on this text in your congregation. What do you think Wesley would say? Why do people continue striving for more, even after they have achieved a reasonably secure, comfortable life?

3. Do you agree that poor people are a sign of who we are rapidly becoming whenever we choose to avoid them in our mad scramble to make it? Explain.

Notes

1. A. Skevington Wood, "Awakening," in *Eerdmans' Handbook to the History of Christianity* (Grand Rapids, Mich.: Wm. B. Eerdmans, 1977), p. 455.

2. Wood, p. 455.

3. Preface to the first *Methodist Hymn Book,* 1739.

4. Quoted in *Eerdmans' Handbook,* p. 447.

5. Tom Sine, *Why Settle for More and Miss the Best? Linking Your Life to the Purposes of God* (Waco, Tex.: Word Books, 1987), p. 3.

3

Christ, the Poor One

CONVERSION TO Jesus Christ and freedom from bondage to self means conversion to a life for others. The biblical terms for *conversion* and *repentance* always imply a turning—a total reorientation. We can never reduce Christian conversion to only one part of this totality. But whenever society pushes us away from poor people, neither do we dare reduce Christian turning until there is no turning back toward them. If poor people have become strangers to us, conversion to our "others" involves a re-turning toward the poor.

The church's renewal of renewals came at Pentecost. Fire and tongues promised to bond many peoples into a new people. Old prejudices, vexing suspicions, gaping distances—God was undoing them all (see Ephesians 2:8-22). Those whom the Holy Spirit touched began living a unified, whole gospel—a gospel of proclamation, communion, and service (Acts 2:42-47).

Such wholeness, such complete turning, had to include those who were poor. Sure enough, those it touched began "selling their possessions and goods, [giving] to anyone as he had need." Throughout the ages, a new relationship with poor people has been part of the renewal of the people of God.

Church Renewal and the Poor

Sometimes poor people have sparked a new relationship with Christ. Giovanni Francesco Bernardone was a popular youth, the son of a wealthy Italian cloth merchant. It was the early 1200s, and young Giovanni was destined to become a knight. But first he made a pilgrimage to Rome. What gripped him there was not the majesty of its cathedrals, but the tragedy of the beggars outside. Moved by compassion, he traded his clothes with one of them and spent the day begging. Soon afterward, he had a vision of himself as the rich young ruler of Matthew 19.

Convinced that the gospel calls Christians to give freely to the poor, Francis of Assisi took that step himself. Eventually he founded a religious order dedicated to caring for the poor and sick. In the growing cities of Italy, Francis shared the gospel with ordinary people, even as he shared their poverty. Today this "Little Brother of Jesus" continues to inspire ordinary Christians with his winsome love for both Christ and the poor.

Sometimes a new relationship with Christ has thrust Christians toward those who are poor. In chapter 2, we saw how this happened to John Wesley. A foremost evangelist of the 1800s was Charles Finney. While calling all sinners to repentance, Finney directed his most forceful message to church people who were living unconverted lives. For Finney, sin was selfishness. Conversion included living for others. Wherever Finney conducted revival meetings, he left behind benevolent societies for every conceivable social ill of the day. Above all, that meant slavery.

Finney denounced the refusal of most churches to take a stand against slavery. He refused communion to slaveholders. Abolitionist societies sprang up wherever he had been. "Revivals are hindered," he wrote, "when ministers and churches take wrong ground in regard to any question involving human rights."[1]

Sometimes both conversion to Christ and conversion to poor people have occurred at once. Such was the case among Anabaptists in sixteenth-century Europe. The movement spread fastest among peasants, who for centuries had lived in near slavery, farming other people's lands.

Civil and religious authorities alike reacted violently when the common people began taking Luther's *priesthood of all believers* seriously, demanding equal access to God, land, power, and human rights. Luther himself drew back from this obvious conclusion. He harshly condemned peasants who found biblical reasons for rebelling against feudal authority in 1525.

Though most Anabaptists rejected the violence of both lords and peasants, they did not draw back from biblical teachings that favored the poor. Separating the social and spiritual consequences of the gospel made no sense to them. Equal access to God implied equal access to the fruit of God's creation.[2]

While drawing its ranks from among society's destitute, the Anabaptist movement also reached out to the neediest. A prominent leader, Menno Simons, could imagine no other kind of discipleship. He asked how leaders of powerful, wealthy churches could dress in "silk and velvet, gold and silver, and in all manner of pomp and splendor," yet allow fellow believers to beg for alms. How could they claim to be the true Christian church while "poor, hungry, suffering, old, lame, blind, and sick people . . . beg their bread at their doors"?[3]

In contrast, wrote Simons, those who are truly converted have their citizenship in heaven. In other words, their allegiance owes nothing to splendid palaces of the earth's powerful. They live *for* others, not *off* others. "They use the lower creations such as eating, drinking, clothing, and shelter, with thanksgiving and to the necessary support of their own lives, and to the free service of their neighbor."[4] If such a gospel meant banishment, prison, torture, and brutal death at the hands of Catholics and Protestants alike, it also brought the Anabaptists closer to Jesus Christ. Like him, they were poor. Like him, they suffered.

In 1539, an Anabaptist woman named Anna faced burning at the stake in her hometown of Rotterdam. As death approached, she penned a riveting letter to her infant son.

"Honor the Lord in the works of your hands, and let the light of the Gospel shine through you," she counseled him. "Love your neighbor" by living honestly, sharing bread with the hungry, and clothing the naked. She urged that he not accumulate material possessions: "[Do not] have anything twofold; for there are always some who lack." What the Lord granted him beyond his needs he should share that very day, and God's blessing would be his.

Above all, Anna implored her son to choose the narrow way that she had followed. She knew the cost all too well. Yet her counsel was clear and firm: "Where you hear of a poor, simple, cast-off little flock, which is despised and rejected by the world, join them; for where you hear of the cross, there is Christ; from there do not depart."[5]

Personal Renewal and the Poor

Joining Christ among people who are poor, getting close enough to hear God's voice in their voices, is still a challenge to us today. But conversion to poor people is also an invitation.

"When we don't live with the people who are poor and don't count them among our personal friends," says Mary Jane Newcomer, "it's well-nigh impossible to relate biblically and wholesomely to the subject of poverty. I consider it my own 'pearl of great price' that God has altered my life to include the perspective of the poor." After all, she explains, poor people have taught her about more than the abstract issue of poverty. Her pilgrimage among them has given her life "firm footing and a faith that is my own."

When Mary Jane first accepted the invitation to join Christ among people who are poor, what she encountered stunned rather than illumined her. As a Mennonite, she shares the same heritage of faith as Anna of Rotterdam. But with four and a half centuries between them, poverty was a distant memory. "We were middle-class, midwestern Americans, conservative in theology, in lifestyle, in worldview, rarely exposed to the reality of poverty in our own small world, let alone the broader world."

Mary Jane had left the broad, lush cornfields of Iowa and was traveling amid the steep, stark cornfields of highland Guatemala. "The scenery in Guatemala is breathtaking and heartbreaking all at once," she explains. "The reality of poverty dots the grandeur of nature."

Her first reaction to stark poverty was to look away. "Upon our arrival in Guatemala, we were whisked off to language study. Dotting the countryside were what I then called hovels. I refused to let my eyes linger on them. Somehow I felt that as long as I didn't see people in those huts, I could go on believing they weren't homes—just stables." But she couldn't look away.

In a few weeks, her family was beginning an assignment with a Christian development agency. She, her husband, and her children were living and working among the K'ekchi Indians. The K'ekchi hold to their distinctive culture with dignity. But they depend on plantation owners for the land to grow food. And they face discrimination or even hatred from Latin, Spanish-speaking Guatemalans. "They've been told in hundreds of ways for hundreds of years that they are inferior, the slaves, the butt of rich men's jokes, to be used for their purposes," Mary Jane explains.

"Poverty faced me every single day from morning to night. I had one of two choices. One, continue to shift my eyes, shield myself from the suffering, and just see masses. It's easier that way. Or I could begin to really see and let these people personally become my friends and teachers.

"That's when Scripture began to take on another twist. I no longer enjoyed verses like Psalm 37:25—'I have never seen the righteous forsaken or their children begging bread.' I saw my brothers and sisters in Jesus dying before my eyes for lack of life's basic needs. I looked into their faces; I heard their stories; and all the rationales and reasons I had for poverty didn't mean anything anymore. All my carefully thought-out theology, worked out on the pews of my church, no longer fit the reality I was experiencing here. Furthermore, I knew the reality wasn't going to change. I had to do the changing."

Change came in different ways—sometimes gradual, sometimes dramatic. Shopping one day for the blue jeans her growing son needed, she found herself calculating their exchange rate in bags of corn that could feed a K'ekchi family. On another day she accompanied a colleague to a rural clinic and helped weigh babies.

While she worked with two other North Americans amid a sea of K'ekchi faces, "childhood images of missionary nurses in African jungles came to mind." But the stereotype of white people saving dark people had long ago lost its hold. "These people certainly don't have *heathen* stamped on their faces," she muttered to herself. Instead she saw friends; and she saw "the face of Jesus in 'the least of these my brothers.' "

Her single most profound experience came when the son of a K'ekchi colleague died of a sprained knee. When the boy's father took him to a hospital for treatment, the Spanish-speaking medical personnel administered placebos and painkillers, not antibiotics. Infection set it, and eventually the boy died. Mary Jane notes, "If he had been my son or the son of a Spanish family, he would never have died. But because he was 'just a K'ekchi,' he did not merit the care that is every person's due.

"That episode more than any other single thing has bonded me to these people in new ways. I have found a deeper commitment emerging from within. I want to walk and live and be among these people in greater solidarity than ever before. And in that solidarity I have begun to see beauty and potential and deep faith emanating from these people. In many ways, I had overlooked it before. I no longer see them as poor people, though at times I am still caught up short at how poor they are. I see them as people far richer than I in matters of faith and practice."

A few weeks later, Mary Jane was sitting in a K'ekchi home at a corn-planting celebration dinner. "We were on low benches, with soup bowls at our feet for lack of a table. The smoky kitchen fire burned our eyes. As we talked, the conversation naturally turned to God, our beliefs, when, why, and how we believed." The pastor turned to Mary Jane and asked what difficulties she encountered in her faith and what made her faith grow.

Having just heard their stories of faith, Mary Jane had nothing to say. "My commitment has never really cost me anything. What do I know about commitment in spite of persecution, racial prejudice, hatred, broken families, economic want? His question continues to plague me. I weep for my poverty of spirit, yet rejoice that these people are rich far beyond my comprehension. I have come to see beyond their poverty and my wealth. Instead, I see their wealth and my poverty. The K'ekchi people have ministered and *missionaried* me."

More recently, Mary Jane reflected: "Little did we know how the last four years would change us." Those years among the K'ekchi "restructured our life, our convictions, and our whole view of Scripture." To illustrate, she tells of reading Galatians 2:9-10, in which the apostle Paul wrote about his mission to the Gentiles.

Paul recalled a crucial summit conference with James, Peter, and John to discuss doctrine and mission strategy. What about the Jewish customs? What about the law of Moses and the sign of circumcision? As the apostles parted, much was still not clear. Yet "those reputed to be pillars, gave me [Paul] and Barnabas the right hand of fellowship when they recognized the grace given to me. . . . All they asked was that we should continue to remember the poor, the very thing I was eager to do."

Mary Jane recalls: "I looked at this passage, and I looked at it, and I said, 'That has never been in my Bible before!' Nothing here about teaching church doctrine, no exhortations on how to evangelize—just 'remember the poor.' If I relegate the poor to Sunday school discussions and conference topics, but don't allow those poor to be my teachers, I miss the whole point of missions. . . .

"Yes, the poor have changed the very nature and form of my commitment to Jesus, how I now read Scripture, and how I define poor. Now that our term is coming to an end here, I find myself praying repeatedly, 'Dear Lord, please don't let me lose the lessons I've learned here. Please put us where the poor can continue to probe and vitalize my faith.' "

Congregational Renewal and the Poor

Conversion to the poor can transform entire congregations, as well as individuals. In the economically depressed Canadian steel city of Hamilton, Ontario, a new kind of church is coming together. Poor and nonpoor are sharing a liberating salvation in Jesus Christ. And Christ is converting them to one another. Social change is beginning amid the most ordinary of congregational activities. The church is called Welcome Inn.

"I was welcomed here in a way that I never thought I could be," says Joyce Lichtenberger, who has suffered economic want during most of her life. "I had such a low opinion of myself, but I walked in here and everyone was saying, 'Welcome! Sit down!' And I thought, 'If you knew me, you wouldn't feel that way.' What I didn't realize at the time is that they did know me. They had seen many people like myself, and it didn't matter. They loved me. They quickly set about telling me that God loved me, which was hard for me to accept."

What surprised Joyce even more, as she accepted God's love and began participating in the church, was that she had something to offer. She had played in rock-and-roll bands for many years and was ready to put music behind her. But the church trusted her to lead in music and encouraged her to write songs glorifying God. Now she is teaching Sunday school besides.

"That's the whole magic of Welcome Inn," Joyce explains. "Nobody's going to say, 'Well, that's not good enough.' Some people, through disabilities, have so little that they can do. But when they do it, it's such an amazing thing."

Hugo and Doreen Neufeld are pastors at Welcome Inn. Hugo notes why it is so important for his low-income friends to contribute to society and to others at church. Many institutions classify low-income people as recipients. "And so it becomes a one-way street. They receive welfare, they receive housing allowance and low-cost housing."

Unfortunately, the same thing often happens in churches. "When low-income people come into a church, they usually don't find a niche in which they can contribute." Instead, "the strongest people contribute in the choir, in the reading of the Scripture, in the pastoring." But where people can read Scripture even if they stumble, or share their struggles coming to church even in a call to worship, they "find a whole new world opening up."

Most members of Welcome Inn are low-income. Perhaps that is because it is easier for those who are poor in obvious ways to expose the struggles in their lives. As Joyce puts it: "It's so easy to hug people when you don't have a mask on." Through poverty and troubled backgrounds, "somehow our coverings have been taken off through life. We've been brought down to a point where the things that really matter are all that's left"—dignity, love of others, love of God, and God's love for each person.

Yet the welcome at Welcome Inn also extends to those with higher incomes. Says Hugo: "We're beginning to experience the richness of someone who comes from a more wealthy background and is able to be stripped of some of their hang-ups and share that with us. A beautiful thing happens within our church here as the rich and the poor share together. Proverbs 22:2 says, 'The rich and poor meet together: the Lord is the maker of them all' [KJV]. And it is God's intention that we meet together. We are all part of the body."

"We need a lot more bridging," says Doreen. "We all have gifts. We all have something to share, and all have something to learn. We need more places, more structures, where we can come together as people and just accept each other as people created in God's image."

Bringing together poor and nonpoor does not rule out confrontation. "The poor are confrontive to people in our society," says Hugo. "At the Welcome Inn, we're experiencing this more and more as we discover that it is God's intention that everyone have equal access to the resources in this world."

People sometimes ask Welcome Inn members what they can do about poverty. "There are poor people in almost every community," replies Hugo. "They are often hidden. But go out there and find them. And listen to what the poor are saying. Become their friends. You may need to get away from the food-hamper image, where you simply go and provide food for the poor. Get out there and listen to them. Who are they? What are their joys? What are their sorrows? How has God worked in their life? How hasn't God worked?

"What would happen in a church of, let's say, two hundred members if fifty of them became personal friends of some of the lowest income people in their communities? We might be really surprised. My guess is that when we become personal friends with the poor, some of the poor would begin asking the deeper questions of life. They are already. They're asking these questions of life even outside the institutional church. And there are Christians out there who have never set foot through a church door. We need to hear some of the experiences the poor have had with God—stories that aren't being told at this point. Some of those stories will come out as we become friends to the poor."

• • •

Learning by Heart

Read Luke 10:25-37, then reread verses 25-29.

The lawyer came to Jesus to test him with a question about eternal life. When Jesus tested him instead, the lawyer posed a second question to shield himself and limit his obligations. But rather than protecting himself, he opened himself up to further scrutiny. And Jesus accepted the invitation.

The lawyer's question, "And who is my neighbor?" was more significant than he realized. Another way to ask it is, "Where do I live?" or "Where do I find life?" Even more pointed is, "Where is my heart?" or "Where is my treasure?"

Put yourself in the lawyer's shoes as he stands before Jesus. A crowd is watching and listening. Who are they? How does Jesus relate to them? Now let the lawyer's question become your question. Speak the deeper concerns that underlie the question "And who is my neighbor?"

• • •

For Thought and Discussion

1. Recall your earliest encounter with poverty, hunger, or racism. (If you were or are poor yourself, recall the first time you realized you were poor.) Have the poor ever *missionaried* you, as Mary Jane Newcomer describes?

2. When you hear the words *church renewal*, what usually comes to mind? Have you ever associated poor people with church renewal before? Have you ever associated poor people with conversion? Have you ever thought of poverty as a place to meet God? What problems do these ideas present to you? What new insights?

3. Generate a list of ways in which you could go about developing personal friendships with low-income people in your local area. Don't evaluate or decide on any one proposal until you have brainstormed a number of ideas. If you are studying this book as part of a group, do this together. Then decide which projects to explore further. What could you do as a group, as individuals, or in pairs?

Commit yourself to seeking out some kind of encounter with poor people during the next six weeks. To help you do so with sensitivity, see "Arranging Encounters Between Middle- and Low-Income Groups," near the end of this book.

• • •

Face-to-Face Encounters[6]

Ana de Garcia and George S. Johnson

Read through the list of face-to-face encounters that follows. Come to the next session ready to identify which encounter you have chosen. Give this serious consideration. There is no substitute for the actual experience. You may propose your own plan and ask for the group's approval.

● I will volunteer to help at a food pantry or soup kitchen two times during the next four weeks. This will include entering into conversation with the recipients.

● I will volunteer (with others) to weatherize the home of a poor family or elderly person(s) and get to know the residents.

● I will volunteer to serve and/or observe an emergency center where the poor are served. Examples might include the emergency waiting room at your county hospital, the courthouse where hearings and trials take place, the food-stamp center, or legal aid office.

● I will visit the unemployment office on two different occasions and enter into dialogue with those making application.

● I will volunteer to go with a social worker or police officer two times on visits that will help me understand the struggles of the poor.

● I will spend one night from 10:00 p.m. until 5:00 a.m. on the streets of an inner city to listen, touch, taste, smell, and feel what goes on and how some people of our society live. (This should be done in pairs or as a small group).

● I will go on a mini (weekend) trip to a third-world situation where face-to-face encounter with the poor is made possible.

● I will arrange for two visits with a refugee or displaced family, one in my home, one in their home, to discuss their struggles, culture, values, and signs of hope.

● I will volunteer to spend a night at an emergency shelter or halfway house and listen to the stories of those needing this service.

● I will visit an Indian reservation, arrange for in-depth conversations with Native Americans or Canadians and those who work with them.

● I will visit a prison on two different occasions and enter into dialogue with inmates with a special focus on poverty, racism, and societal prejudice.

● I will visit with two farm families who have had to foreclose because of economic hardship, seeking to understand and give support.

Notes

1. Donald W. Dayton, *Discovering An Evangelical Heritage* (New York: Harper & Row, 1976), p. 18.

2. Walter Klaassen, ed., *Anabaptism in Outline: Selected Primary Sources* (Scottdale, Pa.: Herald Press, 1981), pp. 234-40.

3. Klaassen, p. 241.

4. Klaassen, p. 109.

5. Thieleman Jansz van Braght, *The Bloody Theater or Martyrs Mirror of the Defenseless Christians Who Baptized Only upon Confession of Faith,* trans. Joseph F. Sohm (Scottdale, Pa.: Herald Press, 1938, 1987), pp. 453-4.

6. From pages 12-13 of *Evangelism and the Poor* by Ana de Garcia and George S. Johnson, copyright © 1986 The American Lutheran Church. Reprinted by permission of Augsburg Fortress.

4

When Did We See You?

FEW OF US think of ourselves as rich economically. But most of us do not consider ourselves poor either. We are simply nonpoor, working hard to get by, then working hard to get ahead. Our eyes are not on a life of luxury, though a few luxury items are welcome. Our eyes are on basic security for ourselves, our children, and our retirement years. Reaching that goal involves enough day-to-day problems. Why take on more?

So poor people easily become strangers to us. Poverty in Canada, the United States, or overseas is someone else's problem. Of course it bothers us. We want to show we care. That is why we donate money to relief, development, or social service agencies. But then it may be all the easier to think of poverty as their problem, not our own. In a way, we have hired the specialists to take care of it.

In Jesus' story of the good Samaritan, robbers mug a man and leave him to die. A priest and Levite pass him by; the Samaritan does not. Would Jesus be able to tell that story today?

The distance between Jericho and Jerusalem is about the distance many people commute these days. Where would the story's shock value be as today's priest or church leader whizzes by on the way to work from the suburbs? Today, we all may pass by. That is what superhighways and expressways are for. We can travel through neighborhoods we might otherwise fear to visit. Even today's Samaritan, with all the best of intentions, might pass by. A blink, and he misses the scene. Another, and the off-ramp is behind him.

A hundred other viaducts and arteries crisscross our society and route us past the poor too. These structures are less concrete, but they are just as compelling—the school system, the news and entertainment media, the workplace, sometimes even churches and volunteer organizations. And affluence itself gives us the ticket to travel this maze of highways to somewhere other than our neighbors who are poor.

But society's structures do not simply ignore poor people and try to steer us elsewhere. They are also the very channels that supply much of what we know, or think we know, about people who are poor. Are the messages they send us fair? Are the images they project accurate? We may never be certain unless we learn to know poor people themselves. That is why in this book we are not just talking *about* poverty.

Poverty is an *issue*—so many statistics about which to have an opinion, debate, and then dismiss as we go on to the next issue. What we are talking about are human beings who are poor. People whose wisdom, foibles, opinions, needs, and vitality would be no easier to ignore than our best friend's—if only we knew them as people. People of immense wealth, even in poverty.

Our task, then, is to read our world, and world poverty, in partnership with poor people. It is to study the Bible with the poor. If we are going to understand and respond to what it says about poverty, wealth, and good news for poor and nonpoor alike, there is no other way.

As often happens, however, learning new skills involves unlearning old habits. It does little good to blame ourselves if society has taught us to avoid poor people. But we will only rediscover our neighbors who are poor if we become aware of the *highways* we have memorized over the years. Then we will be able consciously to steer ourselves along other paths and side streets.

Don't Stereotype Me!

Kerry is an American Indian who lives in Minneapolis, Minnesota. She has two daughters and is on welfare. She admits that being a single parent is what keeps her poor. But she still wants to break down stereotypes about poverty.

Kerry would seem a likely candidate for "getting out of poverty." She has finished high school and held good jobs. In fact, she is halfway through college and has tried hard to finish. The trouble is that when she tried to study and get ahead, the welfare system penalized her. Listen to her story.

"I live in a co-op—low-income housing, subsidized housing. I like the house, but they don't keep it up as well as they should. The thing about it is, I'm real grateful to have it because I couldn't make it without it; but I'm stuck there. I can't move. I can't do anything. I cannot go to school without them cutting into my grant, because they take 30 percent of everything. It's another way of keeping me down. If I want to keep my house, I have to stay poor.

"They are working now in the legislatures trying to cut out the penalties on welfare for going to school. When I called [the welfare agency] and asked, 'How come I only got $300?' she said, 'Well, if you can go to school full-time, you can work full-time.' I said, 'No, right now I can't work full-time and make enough money to support myself. I will just quit [school].' And she said, 'Fine. We don't care.'

"I have a good résumé, and I'm a good worker. I was offered a job last spring. It started at $18,200 a year. It sounded great! Then I broke down what I would need and figured that $18,000 is $1,500 a month before taxes. As soon as I started working, I would get no medical benefits. The government cut that off. The insurance for my two kids is $160 a month. My rent would immediately go up to market price, which is $560; and my day-care came to $600 a month. So right there is $1,100. And that's before you think of food and bills and transportation and everyday necessities like clothes and whatever else.

"I couldn't take it. It didn't even cover my bills. As long as I stay on welfare, I get some subsidies, I get some help. They are a trap. Once you are in, it's so hard to get out. I've worked since I was fourteen years old; so I can get a job anywhere. But because I am a single parent, and there is no day-care available, and [given] the cost of day-care, I can't support myself.

"I believe that everyone should be taking care of everyone else. It's always been an Indian way of life, but the government and the welfare system make that impossible. You can't help other people, you can't live with other people, without getting your benefits cut. You cannot take in your sick brother, your alcoholic brother, or your old grandmother for more than thirty days, because your rent goes to the market rate.

"With what little you have, you can't take care of anyone else, because they're taking food out of someone else's mouth. That's why we have a lot of homeless people. People just aren't able to take them in without fear of losing what little they have. That's real hard. It's a real degrading system too. My first and foremost rule is, 'Do unto others as you would have them do unto you.' You do what you can for other people. It's hard when you can't do for yourself.

"A year ago I could never have told anyone my problems because I've always worked, took care of myself. It's a real blow. It wasn't until this winter I started being able to. I realized how much other people didn't understand. 'Why are you receiving this check when you have an education?' they ask. They just don't understand.

"You may say, 'Well, so many people cheat on welfare.' They do, but it's not to the extent that everyone thinks that it is. I've taken money from my mother. You are supposed to report on all gifts of money so they can take it out of your next month's check. If you work for a day because you have nothing in your house, they'll take it out of your next month's check. A lot of people will do day labor instead of standing in line for food. That's considered welfare fraud.

"No one wants to live on $200 a month. No one can be lazy and live on $200 a month. [People say,] 'They're just laying back and collecting this money.' No one lays back on $200 a month! They can't find a place to stay for $200 a month! If you could find a room [for $200], you would have no money for food, utilities, or clothes, or anything. I don't understand people who think that way.

"I have fears of getting stuck in a rut. I feel it more than ever—the hopelessness. I'm going to tackle school again, but it's real scary. I'll just do the same thing as I did last time. I'll go as long as I can till I can't take it no more.

"When I was younger, I thought that I wanted lots of money and a big house with a swimming pool and a nice car. Now, I just want enough to pay the bills—to never have to worry if there is enough for groceries this week, or do the kids get shoes this month or next? Part of poverty comes with being stuck in a certain place and not being able to do anything about it. The bad part about poverty is what it does to your soul, your self-esteem, and to your whole being."

"Why This Waste?"

Society's highways help us avoid poor people. There are the visible highways that road crews pave, the ones that whiz us to the suburbs. And there are invisible highways as well, the ones that schools, businesses, media, and government bureaucracies lay out.

Sometimes we use the Bible itself as a convenient road map for this invisible highway system. We keep a copy tucked in the glove compartment, so to speak, just in case we make a wrong turn. If we end up in a strange neighborhood—an idea, theology, person, or group that could bring us face-to-face with the poor—we reach for familiar passages of Scripture. Perhaps it is a conscious reaction; more likely not. Imagine that this is your reaction as you read the following text from Matthew 26:6-13:

> While Jesus was in Bethany in the home of a man known as Simon the Leper, a woman came to him with an alabaster jar of very expensive perfume, which she poured on his head as he was reclining at the table.
>
> When the disciples saw this, they were indignant. "Why this

waste?" they asked. "This perfume could have been sold at a high price and the money given to the poor."

Aware of this, Jesus said to them, "Why are you bothering this woman? She has done a beautiful thing to me. The poor you will always have with you, but you will not always have me. When she poured this perfume on my body, she did it to prepare me for burial. I tell you the truth, wherever this gospel is preached throughout the world, what she has done will also be told, in memory of her."

Keep pretending that you are trying to avoid poor people. How would you answer these questions? (1) Why *wasn't* the woman's action wasteful? (2) Why do poor people continue in their poverty? (3) What does Jesus care about most? (4) What do you find in this passage that is comforting?

Now imagine that you are Kerry. How would you answer the same questions if you were her? (1) Why don't you, Kerry, think the woman's action was wasteful? (2) Why do poor people continue in their poverty? (3) What does Jesus care about most? (4) What do you find in this passage that is comforting?

What have you discovered? Were your responses different for the different characters that you put on? Did you see new facets to the Scripture when you read it from the perspective of Kerry, a poor person?

Over the years many people have used this passage, along with its parallels in Mark 14 and John 12, to argue that Christians should not worry much about poor people. "We should be concerned for the poor," they might say. "But we shouldn't let social problems distract us from what really matters— meeting spiritual needs. That's what Jesus cares about. In fact, nowhere in the Bible is that any clearer than here. Resources are limited. The disciples were right about that. But they had their priorities all wrong.

"There will always be poor people. Some people just can't seem to get their lives together. They waste their money on all kinds of vices rather than saving to get ahead. Sin—that's the problem. Jesus died for our sins, and this woman was helping him get ready. She was making a sound investment in the future. Eternity itself was at stake. And that is what we should invest in too."

What might someone in Kerry's situation see in this story? First, I think she probably identifies more with the woman herself than with detached arguments about setting priorities, allocating scarce resources, and making sound investments.

Kerry might say, "The problem with those who manage the world's money purses is that they treat people like objects. That's the real reason people stay poor. Or they overlook them altogether. Women—poor women like me and her—get treated that way most of all. See how quickly the disciples started talking over her head? She wasn't a person to them. She was just part of the furniture. And it happens again and again when religious leaders—mostly men—explain this passage. Maybe they switch things around and ask, 'Why waste money on the poor?' But it's the same thing. And it's not what Jesus did.

"Jesus defended the woman. 'Why are you bothering this woman?' he asked. He paid attention to the woman and her needs. He cares about those of us the world ignores. We have needs that can't wait until eternity. But we don't just want to be objects of charity either. The woman needed to give back to Jesus some of the love he had showed her. She would never be a whole person until she too could take the initiative and act. When she did that, it wasn't a waste to Jesus because *she* wasn't a waste."

You Had to Be There

"Lord, when did we see you hungry or thirsty or a stranger or needing clothes or sick or in prison?" In Jesus' warning of what will come at the final judgment, sheep and goats alike ask this question (Matthew 25:37-39, 44). Both groups are bewildered. The faithful sheep are winning approval for something they didn't know they had done. Meanwhile, the goats seem to be learning of missed opportunities for the first time.

There is real drama here. The king had been present among the poor and needy. Some had served him; others not.

But neither group had noticed him. What made the difference? The sketch leaves the answer as elusive as this king himself. Perhaps, as the expression goes, "You had to be there."

Perhaps the *sheep* had simply become involved with poor people as friends and neighbors. Then they had done what friends and neighbors usually do—help out unselfishly. Maybe their friends and neighbors would return the favor sometime, maybe not. It's just how things ought to be among neighbors. The sheep had helped in everyday ways, never thinking that King Jesus himself was there. But they had let themselves get close to the poor. That was their quiet, workaday heroism.

Where did the *goats* go wrong? The likely reason becomes clearer. It was just as ordinary. If they harbored malice, it was no more obvious than the heroism of the sheep. They just were not around. Maybe they were too busy. Maybe they were afraid to go into strange neighborhoods. Maybe they worried that if they invited "those people" in for dinner, they would stain the tablecloth with dirty elbows. And what if there was nothing in common to talk about? Or, most likely, their paths never seemed to cross. Different accents, different customs, different jobs, different churches, different social classes—society's expressways again.

It takes work to bridge these distances. It can be painful to let go of stereotypes. We may need to train ourselves to listen, really listen, to people we've learned to take for granted. No one may ever anoint our feet with perfume, but what about the unseen women who clean our hotel rooms when we travel? Who are the people earning minimum wages on the other side of the fast-food counter? How can we ever learn to know the people who grow cheap pineapples for us in the Philippines, pick our bananas in Honduras, or assemble our radios in Korea?

You have already started by listening to Kerry. Throughout this book, you will meet others like her from around the world. You will be asked to read the Bible through their eyes. Yes, it may take some practice. To learn to know the poor in real life will take even more work. But there is good news:

Jesus is present among poor people. If we join him there, they might just offer us the good news he has brought to them.

• • •

Learning by Heart

Read Luke 10:25-37; then reread verse 31.

The priest in Jesus' story had good religious reasons for walking by the man on the road. Jesus notes that the robbers had left him half dead. If the priest even thought about aiding the wounded man, a serious doubt would have given him pause. What was before him might be a corpse, in which case the priest would defile himself. The law of Moses placed the priests in different orders, each with their appointed times to officiate in the temple. If this priest got involved with the wounded man, if he had compassion, he might miss his turn, he might lose a holy privilege. Should he risk such (temporary) loss just to save one unfortunate traveler?

In all of us there is some part that seeks to avoid other people's need. Who is this avoider within each one? Spend some time in silent meditation and prayer. Ask yourself, Have I walked by someone in need this week? Have my life decisions—job, place of residence, family decisions—routed me away from poor people? Do I sometimes hide behind holy reasons? What are some ways I have justified "passing by on the other side"?

• • •

For Thought and Discussion

1. Here are some biblical passages that deal with the poor in some way: Deuteronomy 15:11; Psalm 10:1-12; 37:1-11; 37:25-29; Proverbs 6:6-11; 30:7-9; Isaiah 1:15-20; Luke 4:16-21; Romans 12:10-16; 2 Thessalonians 3:10-11; James 5:1-6. For each passage ask, What are some different ways that Christians have interpreted this text?

2. How does the geographic arrangement of my community,

town, or city help keep different economic classes and racial groups apart?

3. What did the school system teach me about poor people? What is it teaching children and youth today?

4. If I lived in a foreign country and all I knew about North America was what I saw in U.S.-made television shows, how would I think North Americans lived? When the poor appear in television and movies, how are they portrayed?

5. What about the news? What kinds of people receive the most coverage? If a news program, magazine, or newspaper does a feature on poverty, hunger, or homelessness, who receives the most attention—poor people themselves or experts discussing their problems? Who gets the last word?

6. Do my sources of news report anything from the so-called third world besides war, natural disasters, drug trade, and corruption? Are features on hunger only about massive famine? Is attention given to causes of hunger?

7. Do poor people feel welcome in the churches I am familiar with? Who does feel welcome? What is the balance between the time and resources my minister devotes to members' personal problems as compared to social problems?

8. What images of the poor do the organizations that appeal for my money present? Are they condescending or do they portray dignity? Do they talk about the causes of poverty? What do they say?

9. Where do my church and I encounter people who are poor and oppressed?

5

Where Your Treasure Is, There Will Your Heart Be

PEDRO WAS ONE of his church's new community development workers. He and I sat chatting in my office in one of
Central America's capital cities as we waited for development
workers from other churches to arrive. "But God's will is that
we prosper," Pedro stated emphatically.

Internally I reacted. He reminded me of a couple I knew.
They were in the market for a good used car and had found
the model they wanted. It was just the right shade of silver
gray. Yet they knew it wasn't God's will. They had prayed for
just such a car—except that it had to have a white interior!

But how could I disagree with Pedro? Wasn't this another
case of bringing different experiences with us when we read
the Bible and finding different messages? I was struggling
against affluence. Pedro was struggling against poverty. The
office in which we sat was actually an *extra* living room in the
house my family rented. Pedro's entire house, in a crowded
neighborhood built a decade earlier for earthquake victims,
would nearly have fit into that one room.

Talking further, Pedro and I agreed. Yes, God does want us
to prosper. But God's will is that we prosper together, not at
one another's expense. As the poor overcome poverty, God
would have them do so in community. Prosperity gained at

the expense of other people, other communities, or even God's creation as a whole is not really prosperity at all. It is an illusion. And judged from God's ageless perspective, it will be short-lived besides.

"The thief comes only to steal and kill and destroy," said Jesus. "I have come that [my sheep] may have life, and have it to the full" (John 10:10). Prosperity, well-being, abundant life, eternal life—the biblical term that sums these up is *shalom*. Often translated *peace,* shalom is really all the "things which make for peace"(Romans 14:19, KJV; Luke 19:42, RSV). It is rich human relationships; material goods adequate to nurture life; cultures with the wisdom to distribute those goods justly; development that does not destroy the creation on which all depend. In short, shalom is wealth at its truest and best.

As human beings, we ought to recognize shalom as our most valuable treasure. And deep in our hearts perhaps we do. God created our true selves for relationship with all other creatures (one more way to describe shalom). But sin has twisted us into selfish selves, in competition with other creatures. It has left us alienated from God, others, and even our own best interests.

Meanwhile, society whispers its own ideas of "peace and prosperity." Too easily we grasp hold of God's biblical promises and twist them to our own selfish ends. Abundance in this life and a better life in the world to come are two such promises. Both can provide a potent, inspiring source of hope as poor people unite to improve their lives. Both can guide the concerned nonpoor as they join them in their efforts.

But whenever we seek to live well apart from others, especially those who are poor, something else tends to happen. In our hands, biblical shalom turns into a prosperity doctrine. This doctrine calls affluence the seal of God's approval and poverty the sign of God's disfavor. Then, to take care of the untidy fact that many righteous Christians are poor nonetheless, we turn the coming of God's new heaven and new earth into lulling reassurances of a better life "in the sweet by and by."

It need not be so. In previous chapters, we have begun listening to people who are poor. Whenever we do so, we allow them to reorder our priorities, help us better understand the Bible, and recognize the myths that distort our view of poor people. It is time we let them revise our notions of wealth as well.

A Wodaabe Elder: Is He Poor?

The Wodaabe people of Nigeria, Cameroon, and Niger would look destitute to many of us. As nomads, they have minimal possessions and no permanent houses. Their survival depends almost entirely on the cattle they raise. They travel long distances, living in camps and avoiding villages.

Yet the Wodaabe enjoy a wealth of which we in modern developed societies know little. Let us listen to one of their elders. Because of his language and culture, most of what he says in reference to men applies to all Wodaabe people. Note also that *Bodaado* means one of the *Wodaabe* people.

"Do you know the *mbodangaaku,* the tradition of the Wodaabe people? This is the way we hold hands with one another. This is the way that we feel that we are attached to each other. The tradition of the Wodaabe is many things. It means that each man should have concern for his neighbor. It means that each man should show his friendship toward others. It means that each man should respect and esteem others.

"Yes, what we call mbodangaaku is many things. It is the many ways of doing things, of behaving, of living. But at its foundation, it consists especially of friendship. It is done when we feel responsibility for each other. We say that our tradition is like a road, like a path. It is the path that God has given to our people. For each one of us, this tradition becomes our sole strength, our sole certainty, our sole security. It is mbodangaaku which gives us life. It is mbodangaaku which allows us to prosper.

"Mbodangaaku is the only wealth of the Wodaabe. It is their true wealth. When we go to the villages of the sedentary people, we are hungry and thirsty because no one gives us anything without money. But when we travel in the bush, wherever there is a Wodaabe camp, we are at home.

"When someone comes to your camp it is because of the tradition of mbodangaaku that you welcome him. Even if you do not like your guest, when his foot comes to your camp, you go to welcome him as if he were your God.

"There is no greater joy than the arrival of a guest who comes in peace and friendship. A guest who comes to your house expresses his friendship to you. By coming he says to you, 'I am your friend!'

"Inside mbodangaaku, my guest is part of me. I must welcome him and give him food. I must converse with him. I must, we say, open the mat for him so that he can sit down. But especially I must open my face to him and show him a heart that is clear and untroubled. And he too, within the bond of mbodangaaku, must bring me his peace.

"When there is a poor man among us, it is the clan which will make him rich. The shame of a single poor man is the shame of the whole clan. How can we live with our herd and be joyful when our brother nearby has nothing with which to feed himself?

"When the clan shows its friendship, its esteem, and its loyalty to a poor man, then the clan also gives him wealth, according to the custom. It is this tradition which enriches the poor man because it is through tradition that we loan him cows, which bind us together. It is the tradition which helps him gain, which enables him to grow.

"The poverty of a Bodaado shows the wickedness of his clan, the meanness of his friends. No one has helped him; no one has loaned him cows. They have left him alone. He is obliged to do [work such as selling firewood or making bricks, which] he is not accustomed to doing, which is not his tradition. And he, left to himself, is obliged to imitate the customs of other cultures and he is not able to follow his own custom.

"Every Bodaado who can follow the path of custom will find great joy and much happiness. He is what he is. We say that he is a free man and that it is the tradition which liberates him."[1]

True Wealth, Deceitful Wealth

What is wealth? The Bible speaks of wealth—or riches, abundance, possessions, treasure—in two ways. In explaining the parable of the sower, Jesus referred to one kind of wealth: The one who received the seed sown "among the thorns is the man who hears the word, but the worries of this life and the deceitfulness of wealth choke it, making it unfruitful" (Matthew 13:22; see also Mark 4:19; Luke 8:14). Proverbs 23:5 speaks of this misleading, false, and insecure kind of wealth in even more colorful language: "Cast but a glance at riches, and they are gone, for they will surely sprout wings and fly off to the sky like an eagle."

Yet the Bible can be just as colorful in celebrating the glory of true wealth. In his letter to the Ephesians, Paul is especially exuberant. He offers praise for the forgiveness of sins "in accordance with the riches of God's grace . . . lavished on us with all wisdom and understanding" (1:7-8). He prays that the Ephesian church "may know the hope to which [God] has called you, the riches of [God's] glorious inheritance in the saints" (1:18).

Paul describes how the cross of Christ has brought estranged ethnic groups—Jews and Gentiles—together in peace, reconciliation, and common neediness before God's throne. This is so that "in the coming ages [God] might show the incomparable riches of [God's] grace, expressed in [God's] kindness to us in Christ Jesus" (2:7; compare 3:8-12).

What emerges in a thorough reading of Ephesians 1-3 is that this true wealth expresses itself in restored, reconciled, and right relationships. God is at work. We are being reconciled to God, who in turn is reconciling once estranged social groups to one another. In describing this drama, Paul's lyrical refrain at every turn is "the riches of God's grace" and "the unsearchable riches of Christ."

Wealth, then, is certainly not evil. Though material wealth is at best tricky and passing, God's wealth heals and lasts. And it is God's wealth that guides us in creating true human wealth.

Therefore, in restoring our own relationship with poor people, it is at least as important to understand wealth as it is to understand poverty. Jesus tells us why: "Where your treasure is, there your heart will be also" (Matthew 6:21).

What we treasure, or value, will determine our life activity as we devote ourselves to one master or another. God or Money, says Jesus, is the usual choice (Matthew 6:24). But not all treasures prove to be of equal value. "Moth and rust" will eventually destroy treasures on earth, if thieves don't get there first (Matthew 6:19). Jesus' counsel then is to invest in the wealth that is lasting: Seek first God's kingdom, God's righteousness, God's justice. Then all the things that other folks lose sleep over—"all these things will be given to you as well" (Matthew 6:33).

If our hearts are set on God's kingdom, receiving material things from God will be something of an afterthought. What will be foremost is living in relationship with God and with all those to whom God draws especially near—the poor, the poor in spirit, the brokenhearted, the hungry, those who weep, the meek of the earth, those who hunger and thirst for justice, the merciful, those with hearts of integrity, the peacemakers, the persecuted, and the oppressed. These are the people Jesus calls blessed (Matthew 5:3-12; Luke 6:20-22). And they are the ones to whom he drew especially near throughout his ministry, as he preached the good news of the kingdom of God.

Now, to those who had trouble sorting out their priorities and choosing this wealth of restored relationships in God's kingdom, Jesus had little choice but to apply shock therapy. To anxious, insecure disciples Jesus said: "Do not be afraid, little flock, for your Father has been pleased to give you the kingdom. Sell your possessions and give to the poor. Provide purses for yourselves that will not wear out, a treasure in heaven" (Luke 12:32-33).

And then there was the rich young ruler who wanted to inherit eternal life painlessly—no doubt the way he had inherited his worldly riches. Jesus confronted him with a blunt choice: "Sell everything you have and give to the poor, and you will have treasure in heaven. Then come, follow me" (Luke 18:22).

But for Zacchaeus, one who truly grasped how much better kingdom treasure could be, the choice was easy. Jesus had no need for tough words about selling possessions. This man knew the shoddy, deceitful kind of wealth all too well. In fact, he volunteered to give up his wealth.

As a tax collector, Zacchaeus's source of monetary wealth was also the source of his spiritual poverty. He was famished for human relationships. As an agent of Rome, he had isolated himself from his own Jewish community. No doubt he worried that he had cut himself off from God in the process. And besides all that, he was short—the easy butt of derision.

If Zacchaeus had gone into tax collecting thinking that people would finally respect him once he had money and the authority of Rome behind him, he knew by now that they had failed him. When Jesus looked up into the sycamore tree, he only had to call Zacchaeus once. The offer of relationship, the chance for true wealth, was an opportunity to jump at (see Luke 19:1-10).

A Heart and Eye Exam

In chapter 6, we will be studying what God's vision for the future offers the poor and how it can shape our current life priorities. First we need to understand the relationship between our vision, our values, and the kind of wealth we invest in. Then we will be in a better position to grasp why it is so important to allow God's vision for the future to shape us here and now.

Our vision for the future and the wealth we seek are always tied together. The future we envision shapes our values. Our values shape our decisions, for we invest in what we value. Wealth of one kind or another is the result we hope for. It will help secure our future. To help us make these connections, let me chart things out.

Vision:
the hopes, dreams
and plans that
together make up
our picture of the
future we seek

Wealth:
the means to secure
our vision of the fu-
ture

Values:
what we believe to be
worth living and work-
ing for, short- or long-
range

**Present
Decisions:**
our investments of
time, energy, and
resources

An example also might help. Here is a common one to which most of us can relate. It concerns our plans for our retirement years:

Vision: Parents see themselves enjoying their children and grandchildren in a pleasant house and yard to which their offspring enjoy coming home. Similarly, a single person looks forward to quality time with nieces, nephews, and close friends.

Values: Time together with loved ones.

Decisions: To have a family; to help children get on their feet educationally and financially; to settle or resettle as near as possible to family and friends.

Kind of wealth: Family relationships; intimate friendships.

Notice that the values and wealth here are practically interchangeable. Somehow the two should relate. They should either be the same, complementary, or mutually reinforcing. Remember the term Jesus used? "Where your *treasure* is, there your heart will be also." Treasure is wealth; to treasure is to value.

Sometimes, however, people's values are one thing, but the

decisions they make and the wealth they seek actually conflict with their deepest values. Or they have conflicting values in the first place. In either case, the result is double vision. That is why Jesus, right after speaking of the treasures we set our hearts upon, spoke also of eyesight (see Matthew 6:22-24).

Even in entirely secular terms, a kind of double vision is possible. What happens if the parents or would-be grandparents become too wrapped up in earning the money they think they need to make their dreams come true? What if they uproot the family repeatedly in search of job promotions? What if they overwork and are too busy for their children when they are young?

Their children may grow resentful. Or the younger generation may simply learn to put their own professional goals above family values, as the parents have done. Either way, when the parents finally retire and have time for family, their children may stay away. Their definition of wealth is too narrow. They are not investing in human wealth—in this case family relationships—along the way.

Of course, some short-term sacrifice is always necessary along the way to any vision worth having. But we dare not let the pursuit of wealth, especially material wealth, become an end in itself. We dare not let it conflict with our ultimate values. That's why it's so important to let God's vision for the future shape our own vision, values, decisions, and definition of wealth.

After all, the most dangerous kind of eye trouble comes when our vision and God's vision are entirely out of line! Our values, decisions, and definition of wealth may all be consistent with each other; but they may all conflict with God's will and God's vision for creation!

• • •

Learning by Heart

Read Luke 10:25-37; then reread verses 33-35.

Most of those listening to Jesus would probably have expected a Samaritan to be one of those to pass by. Certainly

Jesus could have chosen someone more acceptable to be the hero. For the audience, there was no way the Samaritan could be justified. But that was not the point of the parable. Nor was the point to condemn contemporary religious leaders. The whole point of the parable was to say, "Where your treasure is, there will your heart be."

Jesus was saying that station in life or position in society really means little in terms of true qualities of life. So in this parable, the prestigious, the religious, those who were supposed to be close to God, showed that their hearts were far from the heart of God. The one despised by the people of God, the one alienated from the people of God, demonstrated that he and his values were close to the heart of God.

Take a few minutes to become the Samaritan on the Jerusalem-Jericho road. What goes through your mind as you see this stranger who has been stripped and beaten and left half dead? What values compel you to draw close rather than pass by on the other side? What goes through your heart as you care for him by the roadside and as you carry him to safety? What are your concerns as you commit yourself to his long-term care?

Now come back to the present. What transformations of mind and heart need to occur for you to live like the Samaritan today? What treasures, what privileges, are preventing those transformations?

● ● ●

For Thought and Discussion

1. How often do we think of wealth in terms other than money? Why? What does it say about the society that influences us if we have trouble doing so? What are some kinds of wealth that cannot go into a bank account or safe deposit box?

2. It is possible to idealize the traditional lifestyle of a nomadic group like the Wodaabe in Africa until it no longer has anything to teach us. To avoid this danger, consider this question: How would you translate the Wodaabe concept of

wealth into your own culture and society?

3. How does the vision that a person, group, or even a nation has for its future shape its current values, decisions, and view of wealth? What values does each vision below create or reflect? What kind of wealth will people need to secure this vision? What decisions and investments are likely to result?

- A student envisions himself having a good time every weekend and traveling to exotic places whenever he can.
- A businesswoman hopes to live in a community where people help neighbors in time of need.
- A nation dreams of being strong enough militarily to ward off every conceivable threat.
- A congregation envisions a future in which it is large and influential in the community.
- A political movement envisions a better world, but only in secular terms.
- A religious movement promises a better life for the soul in heaven, but only in spiritual terms.

Note

1. Selected and reedited from Angelo Malike, *Beldum: Joy and Suffering Among the Wodaabe,* translated by Cordeen Gorder (Jos, Nigeria: JCMWA/ MICCAO Assemblée, 1984), pp. 20-24. According to the foreword to this book, the Wodaabe are also called the Fulbe or Mbororos.

6
New Heavens, New Earth

GOD HAS A VISION for our future, and the future of all creation. If we make God's vision our own, it will shape our values. If we invest in it, though that involve suffering, it will create its own kind of wealth and security (Mark 10:29-30).

God's vision for the future also has much to do with those who are now poor, those who are now last. Does your vision and mine? If not, our vision of God's will for creation is probably too limited. God is creating a whole new earth and heavens. But confusion about new and old comes as easy as does confusion about first and last. We may miss out on true wealth ourselves. And worse, we may project false promises for the future to those who are poor.

We will do better to let poor people help us sort out what is really new and fresh and what is old and tired. Then together we will be better able to recognize signs of God's "new heavens and new earth" as they break into our world today.

Modern Poverty, Village Wealth

In chapter 5, we noted the danger of twisting God's promise of *shalom* into a *prosperity doctrine* for oneself while postponing prosperity for the poor until a heavenly future. South Africa is a nation where a prosperity doctrine reigns in tragic extremes. It is called *apartheid.*

No one denies that the Afrikaner people, descendants of Dutch settlers, are pious and loyal to their church. After all, they consider themselves God's chosen people. That conviction provides religious justification for the white race to rule South Africa, even though only one person in five is white. It provides the rationale for strict separation of black, white, and colored. And it allows white people to live on the most fertile land, pay lower wages to black people, and prosper amid black poverty. Put simply, apartheid is one community enjoying "God's blessings" at the expense of others.

In the middle of South Africa lies Lesotho, landlocked and mountainous. Though an independent nation, Lesotho depends highly on the white-ruled neighbor that surrounds it on all sides. In South Africa white people can expect to live seventy years and black people fifty-nine years, but in Lesotho black people can only expect to live fifty-one years. Per capita income in Lesotho is only $400 a year, a tenth of what it is in South Africa. To work, many migrate to South Africa for months, years, or decades.

By most yardsticks Lesotho is poor. Yet when a U.S. church worker living in rural Lesotho went looking for someone in his village who could describe poverty, the results were surprising. Only a handful of people thought of themselves as poor. Those who did had sharply contrasting reasons, but one thing in common. They were the ones who looked to South African prosperity for income. After all, in spite of its treatment of blacks, white-controlled South Africa is the place to look for work in shiny, new, modern industries.

Simon Lebusa Nenese had worked in the mines of South Africa for thirty-five years. Now old and sick, he was destitute. Wages had not been fair. What little he had managed to save was gone. A pension the mining company once promised had never come through.

"I am sick; I have no health. My chest—they took X-rays of it there at the mines. My chest hurts a lot. And I have no money; we are hungry. When someone is sick and old like I am, people leave you behind. My family doesn't help. And in the village over there, they don't help. Right here, these people [one niece and her neighbor] help me—only here. There is no peace. Each person makes their own laws. They don't think about others. If your house wall falls down, that is your business. They don't help."

Traditionally, African village life would be kinder to the elderly. In other times, it respected them highly; and in other places, it still does. But with the modern Western economy of nearby South Africa come modern ways.

Lineo Mofokeng reflects the changes. She is a high-school student. Her older brothers work in Johannesburg, South Africa, and send money home. One moment she says she prefers village life, but in the next moment she talks glowingly of going to work in the city. Of one thing she is certain. She knows she does not want "the old ways." She wants what she sees in glossy magazines from South Africa. Let's listen:

Question: Sometimes old people say, "Kids today, they lose the old ways. They only study in school. They don't want to know the old ways." Is that true, or not?

Lineo: Right now, we don't want the old things. There's no use knowing the old things—about animal skins. We don't wear them. And we don't follow the customs. They are hard, and there is no reason to keep them. People used to sit and sleep on the ground on a skin. They didn't have soft chairs. They didn't have hi-fi's.

Q: You like hi-fi's and sofas?

Lineo: Yes, and houses with rooms. I like water systems piped right into the house.

Q: Is there anything of the old ways that you want to keep? Or do you want to change everything?

Lineo: I want to change everything.

Q: Even the food?

Lineo: Yes, and food. We know about protein and vitamins. They used to eat sour sorghum porridge morning, noon, and night. I want a variety. Morning I will eat soft porridge and cookies, cakes. Midday I'll eat meat and rice. In the evening I'll make tea.

Q: Where do cookies come from, or tea?

Lineo: Tea? I don't know. It comes from overseas, right?

Q: Yes, it comes from far away. The foods of this place—cornmeal and greens and meat—are still here. But soft porridge, it comes from the store. You're going to need a lot of money to eat that way. Will you find enough money to eat that way?

Lineo: Yes, I will find it. I want to teach.

Q: What do you lack here? What does your family need?

Lineo: We are needy! We are poor!

Q: You are poor? You sit there nicely on your sofa, with your hi-fi here, and you say, "I am poor?"

Lineo: These were bought. People can sit nicely. The money is gone. It doesn't come.

Q: What about this village? What does it need?

Lineo: Here, we need toilets. And we need to plant trees so we don't have to go so far for firewood. [We need] stores, a supermarket, a liquor store—lots of things.

Q: Would you say you are rich or poor or ordinary?

Lineo: What do you say we are?

Q: I think you are rich. I don't think there is another house as big as this one in the village.

Lineo: [Laughter] We're not rich; we are needy! We'll be rich when I finish my senior year of high school and start to work.

In contrast to Lineo Mofokeng, Teboho Julius Mothabeng is a satisfied man. He is a stonecutter and a mason. He would look poor to most North Americans, but he owns a field and about fifty goats. True, he has known his own share of troubles. His only daughter died as a child. And a few years ago, a car hit him, leaving one arm weak. Still, "As long as I have my hands," he says, "I'm a rich man." Perhaps it is because he has not abandoned neighborly village ways. Listen again:

Question: So how is your life and health?

Teboho: Hey, I'm doing fine. Only thing is, there's a weasel around here. My neighbor's chickens are being eaten. I'd like to make something to put an end to that weasel. Otherwise, we're doing just great. We have built mutual understanding and sympathy; we are like the children of one family; we are around one fire.

Q: You what?

Teboho: We share the fire. In our language that means we see that there is justice among us. If I have nothing, someone gives. If another has need, someone shares with them.

Q: Oh, you share. Everyone here does like that?

Teboho: Even if you go a long way from here, and you say, "Help me," they will help you. Of course, there are some who refuse to share; but as a rule we aren't like that. It isn't our way. There are some who refuse the needy. But that isn't love. Love, that means to help each other. Here we live in peace.

Q: What is peace?

Teboho: When things are fine, that's peace. But we say that peace is something we must mold and form, like clay. We're making peace here. There are people here who ruin peace, who ruin understanding. But we here, we're still building. Yes, there are some children of God who are hungry. If they come and I am cooking, they say, "Can you give me some flour?" If there's some here, I give them some so they can cook for their kids.

Q: Kids today, Basotho youth today, do they still learn the things they need to know to live well?

Teboho: Some still learn. Some don't want to learn anything. It's bad! When their grandfather dies and their father dies, then they don't know the old customs of their home. To know those things is to have a great blessing. For the loss of the traditions, they will fare badly. Like the son of my younger sister—he went to Bloemfontein [in South Africa]. When he came back, he didn't know the customs. He didn't even know how to slaughter a goat. Now he isn't from Lesotho; he isn't from Cape Province; he isn't from anywhere now.

Q: Are you satisfied with the life here? Do you find that the chiefs divide the fields well, that people help each other here. Are you satisfied?

Teboho: The fields aren't divided well. The problem is that the tribe has grown and outgrown the fields. It is not the fault of a person. God just gave us too few fields. But that is why we Basotho must be wise. I am a person who lives by his hands, right? As long as I have my hands, I'm a rich man.

Recognizing Signs of the Kingdom

From God's ageless perspective, the new impersonal ways of modern society are probably getting old real fast. Meanwhile, the larger our stake in that society, the greater may be our surprise when God does something really new.

As author Tom Sine notes, if you ask many Christians what God's future will be like, they speak of heaven, angels, harps, and spiritual bliss. Yet the apostle Paul was emphatic that just as Christ was raised bodily, so will God's children be transformed or raised with new bodies (1 Corinthians 15; Philippians 3:21). How seldom we grasp the astounding implications of this doctrine!

God wants to do more than just save our souls. God wants to save *us*—whole people—spirit, soul, mind, and body. But we cannot be whole apart from others. We are people who form and are formed by communities. Our communities knit together the network we call society. Creation is the nurturing home for all people, communities, societies, and all other life as well.

Does this mean God intends to redeem all of creation? Yes!

Christ came preaching the good news of a kingdom where God reigns. As the book of Hebrews explains, throughout the ages heroes of faith have looked for "the city with foundations, whose architect and builder is God" (Hebrews 11:10). A city is a unit of human society. Foundations fuse it firmly with the earth. Yet this city is heavenly as well, for in it, God's will is "done on earth as it is in heaven."

Both Old and New Testaments speak of God's future as nothing short of "a new heaven and a new earth"! One of the fullest pictures of this new reality is in Isaiah 65:17-25. Where creation is healed and restored, its nurturing fruits are available to all. Poverty is no more. Take a minute to read this passage in your Bible.

If we read the Bible from the perspective of the poor, we will find much cause for rejoicing in Isaiah's vision. Think for a moment. What hope would jump out at you if as a poor person you read Isaiah 65 or Revelation 21? Read it again, imagining that you are the mother of four malnourished children and have lost three more to dysentery and measles before they reached a year. Imagine that your father had supported his family by farming a small tract of land but lost it when a foreign company claimed it owned the title and began growing pineapples for export. Imagine that when you started organizing other women in a shirt factory to press for decent wages, members of your committee lost their jobs and plainclothes policemen singled you out for a beating.

Of course, there are poor people who read the Bible from the perspective of those the world calls rich. I hate to pick on our friend Lineo from Lesotho, since she is still struggling to find her place in the adult world. But her family and friends— as well as faraway economists, politicians, and managers—are making some decisions for her. One result could be that when she is an old woman, her family will be fragmented, her life's labor exploited, and there may be no one to care for her. But even if she fares better under the South African economy than did Simon Lebusa Nenese, will she exchange true wealth for a few consumer items? Will her family trade its African birthright for a bowl of lentil stew? If so, it will be because they have pursued a dubious vision of a better future.

Lest we judge Lineo too harshly, however, what about us? Life in middle-class North America is the envy of people around the world. Never mind that they may only know an idealized version of that life. The television shows, radios, magazines, and popular music that our culture invented are what have flooded the world with that vision of the future.

Yet if all nations were rich in the way we tempt them to become, the world would already have depleted the oil, minerals, topsoil, forests, clean water, and landfill space that sustain our lifestyle. The future that the so-called developed countries are developing will mean an old heaven and an old earth indeed—polluted skies, exhausted land, poisoned waters.

What if we had welcomed the simple pleasures and true wealth of God's heaven and earth all along? Once before, heaven and earth were new. Why should we who are fast wasting creation expect God to renew it now? Only to give the poor another chance to "enjoy the works of their hands" (Isaiah 65:22). Only because God yet longs to rejoice and "take delight in my people" (Isaiah 65:19).

Simon Lebusa Nenese will recognize and welcome the new heavens and new earth when he sees it. Teboho Julius Mothabeng will too. Simon will recognize God's new order because it will be everything his impoverished life on the old earth is not. Teboho will recognize it because he is already welcoming it as he "shares the fire" with others in his village. What he calls the old ways will actually fit into God's new earth quite well. The kind of wealth he treasures now is building a storehouse in the coming kingdom. In fact, it brings the kingdom all the closer as the ways of the new heavens and new earth begin breaking in.

For us to welcome and invest in the new heavens and new earth, we must learn to recognize and strengthen those places where kingdom ways are already breaking in. We also must learn to see the old heavens and old earth we now live in for what they are. Our society is adept at blurring old and new. We are used to "revolutionary" cleansers and "new and improved" deodorants. But inside the slick package, the formula is usually the same old thing.

Of course, we are not God. Our judgments about what is truly old and new in our midst should not be hasty. And when we reach them, they will still only be hunches. God will have the last word. But, still, we should be attentive to the signs of the coming of the kingdom of God and share in that inbreaking wherever we can.

•   •   •

Learning by Heart

Read Luke 10:25-37; then reread verses 31-34.
Two kinds of spirituality are evident here. One is old and

common; the other new and original. One maintains the status quo. The other looks forward in hope as it rebuilds human life.

Which spirituality appears more religious? Why? Which spirituality is most authentic? What makes it so? How would you recognize each kind of spirituality today? Identify real-life examples of both.

We are now roughly halfway through the chapters that make up part one. This might be a good time to take stock of what you are learning. Divide a sheet of paper into four sections. Write one of the questions below in each section. Spend a few minutes in silent meditation focusing on each question. Summarize your meditation with a single sentence in the corresponding section of your paper.

● What am I beginning to learn about the Bible, poor people, and myself?

● What new attitudes is God trying to create in me?

● What are the fears and apprehensions that hold me back?

● How might God want me (us) to express my (our) concern for poor people in new ways?

Close this time of meditation by praying the Lord's Prayer slowly and mindfully, so that the meaning of these familiar words can sink in.

● ● ●

For Thought and Discussion

1. Compare what the Bible says about the new heavens and new earth with an example of how people treat what we might call the old heavens and old earth. First Kings 21:1-19 provides a vivid comparison, especially in the bright light of Isaiah 65:17-25. Read these two texts. How is the earth treated in each? Who enjoys the fruits of the land in each? How are people treated? What role does God play in the Isaiah text? What role would the powerful like God to play in 1 Kings 21? In 1 Kings 21:17-19, God has the last word. What does this

tell us about the relationship between earth and heaven even now?

2. How are the ways of the new heavens and new earth already evident in Teboho's community in rural Lesotho?

3. The questionnaire near the end of the book provides a tool for beginning social analysis. Individually or with a group, answer the questions in it to the best of your knowledge. If you find gaps in your knowledge, ask why that is. If you are reading these chapters on your own, decide how you are going to fill in the gaps. If you are working with others, you should probably work together to answer all the questions in a more thorough manner. Pool ideas about where to find the answers. Then divide up the questions among all participants, and plan to report back in your next session.

This simple survey will not rush you to make judgments that only God can make. But once you have worked through it, you will be in a better position to answer two sets of questions from a faith perspective:

• What are the realities around us that conflict with God's vision of new heavens and new earth? What are the injustices we should prayerfully and prophetically oppose?

• What community organizations and groups are already working in ways that reflect and welcome God's new heavens and new earth? What efforts among the poor in our community should we celebrate? What efforts should we learn from as we develop our own response to the poor? What efforts should we join?

7

Good News to the Poor

ACCORDING TO the apostle Paul, Jesus said this about handouts: "It is more blessed to give than to receive" (Acts 20:35). The proverb suggests why much confusion surrounds donations to poor people. It makes us feel good, even blessed, to give. But because giving can feel so good to us, we must always be careful that our gifts do not humiliate or even destroy those on the receiving end.

If survival itself is at stake, a handout can give life and communicate love. Victims of 1988 floods that covered two-thirds of Bangladesh expressed wonder upon receiving hand-made blankets from North American Christians. They would have been grateful for machine-made blankets too, but they sensed care and respect in these gifts.

Handout after handout, however, will eventually convey a message at odds with love. It will say, "You failure! You'll never be able to help yourself, will you?" No one really wants to live off the dole. Yes, there are those who seem to feel no shame in begging time after time. But look closely. They are usually people so downtrodden, so exploited, so abused, that a basic part of their humanity seems lost. Injustice and neglect have robbed them of dignity.

Amid confusion about handouts, funny things happen.

"Liberals" preach about society's responsibility for the needy. But sometimes they spawn huge bureaucracies that dispense "solutions" to the poor. "Conservatives" preach free enterprise and the power of individual initiative. But they tend to get nervous when poor people start organizing, taking initiative, and claiming power. One approach makes government a charitable organization. The other is confident that individual, private charity will do the job. But neither approach shows much trust in poor people themselves.

Well, what about Jesus? What was his approach? When Jesus preached "good news to the poor," was it a handout? When he put this gospel into practice by giving sight to the blind, mobility to the lame, cleansing to the lepers, hearing to the deaf, and new life to the dead—were these handouts?

In texts like Matthew 11:4-5, the gospel writers present such actions as signs that the kingdom of God is breaking in on human affairs. They are signs that Jesus is the Messiah, through whom the kingdom is coming. And as signs, they show what the kingdom is all about. Just as Isaiah predicted, the kingdom and the new Servant-King make a special place for society's poorest and neediest. In Luke 4:18-19, Jesus took that vision as his own mandate when he quoted from Isaiah 61 to inaugurate his ministry.

Can signs of the kingdom such as these demean their recipients? Of course not. Will the gospel rob poor people of dignity and thwart their initiative? Hardly. Even when Jesus' miracles were in some sense handouts, he gave wisely, in a way that dignified and empowered the needy.

Yet the approaches Christians have made to poor people sometimes have demeaned them and thwarted their initiative. Though full of good intentions, sometimes the church has carried subtle messages at odds with the gospel: "civilization for the savages," or "uplift for the downtrodden." Even "development" can imply a value judgment. Unless we are careful, we communicate superiority, not solidarity; condescension, not compassion; paternalism, not empowerment.

When we begin to share Jesus' concern for poor people, we must also learn from his way of relating to them. Now, more than ever, that means listening to them.

Here Everyone Can Participate

Good news *to* the poor is good news *for* the poor only as it is good news *with* the participation of poor. Christ empowers them to become active participants in the kingdom, active builders of the justice that is its way.

For all his mighty power to heal, Jesus could do few signs of the kingdom where people lacked faith. Mark 6:5-6 says of a visit Jesus made to his hometown: "He could not do any miracles there, except lay his hands on a few sick people and heal them. And he was amazed at their lack of faith."

That should tell us something. But once again, it is easy for people who are not poor to miss the Bible's intention. Our tendency is to think of faith as a creed to which we give mental assent. Or perhaps it is mental calisthenics we think we must go through if we want God to answer our prayers. For the poor, faith must be much more concrete—and so must its fruits.

In working even the mightiest miracles, Jesus asked the needy to participate. To help us in a study of two examples from the Gospel of John, let us invite a guest to join us from Brazil.

Eurides Cruz Nunes is a widow with five children. She works as a nurse, a low-paying job in Brazil. She lives in a housing complex on the outskirts of one of the country's industrial centers, São Paulo. She is active in the health-care workers' union and is a lay leader in the Catholic Church. In that role, she helps struggle for decent local health care, and she plans worship in her parish. Most important, she has helped form a few of the hundred thousand "grassroots Christian communities" that have sprung up among Brazil's poor in the last thirty years.

"The difficulty of our people is unemployment, little health care, and poor housing—in sum, social injustice. When we do find work, it isn't enough to buy our food!

"Faith is important for us to find strength to confront this difficult reality. When we don't have faith, we don't believe that reality can change. I don't have time to stop and make great prayers, but I believe that our prayer is our suffering

lives, our day-to-day work and struggle. I believe God listens
to the prayers of the people. The Word of God tells that God
was faithful to his promise and chose a poor, massacred, hum-
bled people to walk with. Because of this, we're ready to confront our problems and fight for a better life without getting
discouraged.

"The Bible revolves around the great love of God for his
people who are suffering and struggling. We look at this history of salvation repeating itself in every age and never lose
this thread of faith.

"In our grassroots Christian communities, we live like a
family and reflect together on the Word of God. We discover
together the needs of our street, our neighborhood, our people. We make the Word of God a mirror to help us see our
situation. Our grassroots community is a church with the face
of the people. We tend to say it is a "new church," but it's
not new! This is the church of all times. It's the church of our
time, of our reality. When we worship together, we celebrate
our whole life—our struggles, our difficulties, and our vic-
tories.

"The grassroots communities give everyone a voice inside
the church. Everyone has their chance, their opportunity, their
moment. Our communities are no longer the traditional, cen-
tralized church where the priest was the center of attention.
It's no longer a church of dominators. It's the church of Jesus
Christ with the face of the people.

"Most grassroots movements for social change start with a
few active lay people who have a vision of community. It's
only through the commitment of the laity in the church that
grassroots movements gather strength.

"As for faith and politics, Jesus always preached justice. He
was always on the side of the little ones. What we see in Jesus' day, we see in our day as well: the powerful oppress the
little ones. How are we going to live the gospel of Jesus,
which speaks of justice, if we don't struggle against the injustice of today? To live in faith, we have to confront those with
power. There's no other way out.

"I can't live the gospel without joining the struggle of the people—struggling for better transport, decent working conditions, for the right to have an honest union. If I want to live my faith, I can't keep my eyes and ears closed and turn away from all the injustices."

Faith, Action, Mud

When needs are concrete and immediate, faith must be concrete and immediate as well. "Suppose a brother or sister is without clothes and daily food," wrote James. They need more than a *God bless you* or a *Jesus is the answer.* "In the same way, faith by itself, if it is not accompanied by action, is dead" (James 2:14-17). Reading these words we naturally picture a *have* and a *have-not,* a rich person and a poor person. We envision a one-way flow of resources, at least if the rich person will heed the words of James. But we might imagine another kind of exchange as well.

The exchange is mutual as poor people combine their resources of spirit and organization. Picture poor people gathering together, uniting to help one another, joining forces to improve their community or resist injustice. They too discover a concrete faith. Faith in God means faith that their unjust, suffering reality can change. It means faith in one another. It means faith that the tiniest, local actions will matter.

The Gospel of John recounts two parallel healings. Both involve a pool. Both take place on the Sabbath. Both fuel a growing debate between Jesus and the religious leaders in Jerusalem about Jesus' authority. Both bring Jesus and his movement closer to repression. And both depict concrete acts of faith. In one, however, faith falters.

John 5 tells of a disabled man who had waited thirty-eight years for healing by the Pool of Bethesda. Tradition was that an angel occasionally stirred up the waters, and the first one into the pool would find healing. But the man was paralyzed in more ways than one. He had also let paralysis take over his mind and spirit. When Jesus asked him whether he wanted to be healed, he answered, "I have no one to help me into the pool when the water is stirred. While I am trying to get in, someone else goes down ahead of me." He said nothing about his own wants. He never answered Jesus' question directly.

Maybe the paralytic thought his needs were obvious. Yet his answer revealed the shackles that poverty, neglect, and oppression slowly inflict *inside* many who are poor. Fatalism, low self-image, and a chronic sense of dependency are the ultimate injustice they suffer. They see angels and other donors as their only hope. In self-pity the paralytic groans, "No one does it for me!"

Fortunately, he had not entirely lost his dignity and will. "Get up! Pick up your mat and walk," said Jesus. And in a flash of faith, before old patterns could catch up, he followed Jesus' concrete instructions.

Yet years of dependency had taken their toll. The religious leaders quickly discovered him carrying his mat on the Sabbath. They questioned him; and before the authorities, he cowered—"That man, he told me to do it!" His deeper paralysis remained. And later, when he met Jesus again, Jesus urged him to break his pattern of sin. But instead of joining the community of Jesus' followers, he turned informer.

Something quite different happens in the second poolside healing. In John 9 the backdrop is similar, and not just because the Pool of Siloam is nearby. Fatalism infected the scene here too. But this time it was Jesus' own disciples who voiced it. Their faith was in a God who is vengeful, or even fickle. The man born blind expressed a genuine, vibrant, and clearer faith in Jesus, the ultimate expression of God's love for the world.

Brazilian Christians like Eurides like to say, "Our word for prayer is *oração*, which means to pray (*ora*) and enter into action (*ação*)." Think about this as you read the second poolside incident from John 9. Imagine that you live in one of the shantytowns that circle all of Brazil's major cities.

You were born in the countryside, but your family never had enough land to prosper. You heard that jobs were abundant in the city and moved here. But so have millions of other people. If you find work, it pays poorly. As a Catholic, you have gone to mass and prayed to the saints. But now, a Catholic laywoman, Eurides, has invited you to a new kind of meeting. You gather with a few others in a shack of corrugated metal, wood scraps, and plastic. It is much like your own dwelling. Eurides reads the story of the blind man's healing and starts to ask questions. How would you answer?

● Jesus' own disciples thought the blind man was suffering because he or his parents had sinned. Why do we suffer, according to some people? What has the church been saying? What are the real reasons?

● Jesus took mud and told the blind man to wash it out if he wanted to be healed. Why? Was he making a magic cure?

● We know a lot about mud in this neighborhood. In the rainy season it feels like mud is the only thing we have in abundance! What are some of the ordinary things in our neighborhood that Jesus could use to transform our community?

● How did the authorities treat the blind man after he was healed? How do the authorities treat us?

● What are the different ways the man showed he had faith? How will we show we have faith?

Will You Join Us?

Jesus makes at least one other point in the John 9 narrative: The ones who are really blind are the religious authorities, the people with power. Perhaps North American Christians have more in common with them than with the blind man. Let's put ourselves in the shoes of the religious authorities for one moment.

A man, no longer blind, stands before us. He speaks confidently of what Jesus has done for him.

The poor stand before us. They tell of their own miracles. They have recovered dignity as they name injustices. They have discovered community as they organize themselves. They are finding hope that their world—and our world—can change.

We are not used to the poor speaking so boldly. We could react, accusing the man born blind of arrogance and disrespect. We could reject the poor, expel their witness, label it as subversive, as mere ideology.

Or we can do something else. Imagine that a handful of the Pharisees had allowed the man to "evangelize" them, who were so used to lecturing the "ignorant" masses (John 9:34). What a different turn the conversation would have taken!

The blind man asks, "Do you want to become his disciples, too?"

The poor of our world ask, "Will you join us in our efforts to build a more just world?"

It is the moment of truth. We *do* want to become his disciples. We *do* want to make a difference in society. But how?

Another lay leader in a grassroots Christian community in Brazil had this message: "I'd like to say to our wealthy brothers and sisters that salvation doesn't come only for the poor, but for the rich as well." He asked North Americans to share their wealth, happiness, and knowledge with the suffering and exploited. "Tomorrow we too could have a little more equal society."

This same man, running a tiny broom-making shop in a Brazilian shantytown, expressed surprise: "I've heard foreign missioners say that in the U.S. there aren't grassroots communities or people organizing for change like we have."

Clearly, that would be his answer to the question of how. Though he asked for the help of the nonpoor, he is no beggar. His dream is that those who are poor and those who are privileged share together their respective kinds of wealth: "I also believe that the poor have a lot to share with the rich."

Are you ready to take such steps? Are you ready to put faith into action? Are you ready to join with others in a grassroots community for change?

• • •

Learning by Heart

Read Luke 10:25-37; then reread verses 33-35.

As we meet each character in Jesus' story, we learn least about the man who fell into the hands of robbers. After all, had Jesus described the man or revealed his identity, the lawyer might have concluded that only people of that particular type deserve neighborly treatment. All we know is that he was a victim, he was oppressed.

The victim also was totally helpless. He had been stripped, beaten, and left half dead. Obviously his situation is one in which a handout is appropriate. It is sometimes easier *for us* to help people who are destitute than it is to help those who are actively struggling against oppressive forces. We don't have to deal with them as whole people when we are clearly in a position of giving a handout. We need to deal truthfully with ourselves. Even when the victim's need does call for a handout, the Samaritan goes out of his way to empower him. List his ways of doing this.

Now, as you read verses 33-35, put yourself in the place of the Samaritan. The first thing the text says about you is that when you see the victim, you have *compassion* (KJV). Apparently it is this compassion that makes you respond to the victim differently than did the priest and Levite. The text does not say what *they* felt. Could they have felt condescending *pity*, even though they did not act on behalf of the victim? Could you, the Samaritan, have had *compassion* and still not acted on behalf of the victim? As a Samaritan, what in your experience might be the source, the wellspring, of your compassion?

If you are studying in a group, divide into three smaller groups. Each read one of the following texts: Isaiah 61:1-4, 8-9; Luke 7:18-30; Matthew 4:17-25. Then discuss these questions: What signs of the kingdom are evident in this passage? Are the poor passive recipients? How do they actively participate in these demonstrations that the kingdom is breaking in? How does Jesus empower them to do so?

• • •

For Thought and Discussion

1. In his book *Evangelism: Doing Justice and Preaching Grace* (Zondervan, 1982, p. 28) Harvie M. Conn writes: "Those not

on the rolls of the church, the unchurched, do not reject the church because it preaches 'good news.' They reject the church because they have been learning more 'bad news' than 'good news.' " What made the announcement of God's kingdom be good news to the poor? How should Jesus' way of being with the poor influence our own efforts on behalf of the poor?

2. If the poor must be active participants in bettering their own lives together and discovering signs of the kingdom, how might their efforts challenge, surprise, or threaten us?

3. Think of the efforts to alleviate poverty that we know most about. Do they attempt to unilaterally take something good *to* the poor? Or do they seek to create good news *with* the poor?

4. Under what circumstances are handouts appropriate and helpful? Under what circumstances are they inappropriate and hurtful? How can relief efforts meet the immediate needs of poor people without humiliating them?

5. In a grassroots Christian community in Brazil, faith in Jesus means action for mutual aid and social justice, identification with others in the community, and willingness to take a stand. These are some of the things such a group might discuss as it studies John 9 (see pages 94-96). Now answer for yourself, in your own community: How have we been blind? What is the ordinary stuff, the mud, that Jesus could use to heal us? And to meet the needs of the poor in our community? What reactions should we expect from those with power?

6. In chapter 3, I suggested that you seek out a face-to-face encounter with poor people in your area. Have you followed through? If not, look back to question 3 at the end of that chapter. Plan to do one of the activities in the next three weeks.

8

Learning to Read with the Poor

IN CHAPTER 3, Mary Jane Newcomer in Guatemala and members of the Welcome Inn congregation in Hamilton, Ontario, shared their testimonies of conversion to the poor. But such testimonies are just as powerful when they take place *among* poor people themselves. In Latin America, some Christians sing this song:

Cuando el pobre crea en el pobre	When the poor believe in the poor
ya podremos cantar libertad.	freedom we start to sing.
Cuando el pobre crea en el pobre	When the poor believe in the poor
construiremos la fraternidad.	we are building fraternity.
Cuando el pobre anuncia al pobre	When the poor announce to the poor
la esperanza que El nos dió	the hope God gives to us,
es que el Reino entre nosotros nació.	the kingdom among us has been born.

Throughout South and Central America, small grassroots Christian communities—sometimes called *base ecclesial communities*—are offering new life to the Catholic Church. In the same way, John Wesley's clubs and societies for Bible study, prayer, and discussion among England's poor once offered new life to the Anglican Church. As Eurides Cruz Nunes explained in chapter 7, "The grassroots communities give everyone a voice inside the church."

It is a voice that speaks to us also. It invites us to rediscover the power of the gospel by reading the Bible together with those whose need is greatest—those who hunger and thirst for justice. We have already begun. But if we look closer at what we have been doing, perhaps we can make this way of reading a lifelong habit.

What Lamps Are Really For

In Brazil alone there are over 100,000 of these grassroots communities. In the mid-1960s, mission teams and parish priests began promoting the groups. While the church has provided vital training to lay leaders, groups inevitably develop their own identity. Exercising their own leadership in their own way is an important source of dignity and renewal in a church where for centuries the poor often were merely passive consumers of the sacraments.

Prayer and Bible study are at the heart of community life. Many groups meet together simply to strengthen their religious life. Others go on to become what one observer calls communities of mutual aid. These kinds of groups initiate activities to improve their neighborhoods, sanitary conditions, medical services, bus transportation, or schools.

Discovering deeper causes of poverty, still other groups become communities for social justice that work for social, economic, or political transformation. But discovering what the Bible means for their community life remains central.

Their method of Bible study is simple, yet profound: *Read the Bible. Read the world. Relate the two. Respond.*

The results of Bible study within the grassroots communities can be astounding. Perhaps that is because the simplicity of the method cuts away so many pretensions. Or perhaps it is because the conditions of the poor allow so few pretensions in the first place. The settings are not theological ivory towers. The settings are not carpeted Sunday school rooms. The settings demand that the Bible speak to concrete human need, or it won't be good news at all.

"It's from our shared suffering that we raise communities and work for change," explains one participant. "Because of God, people believe that our misery will be transformed. Since God is in the midst of the poor, we can work to obtain a better life. We meet together in our community and look to God to liberate us from our problems. The Bible is the most important part of the Brazilian church's journey."

Antoinha Lima Barros is a twenty-one-year-old teacher. She lives in Para, northeast Brazil. Her father, a field hand, was recently murdered. Since her mother works as a low-paid maid, Antoinha is now the chief breadwinner for her family of six. She is the only family member who has been able to study, but she still earns a minimum wage. Antoinha is active in grassroots communities and youth groups, as well as in labor and land movements. She emphasizes that her political activism grows intimately from prayer and the Bible.

"The Bible is so important to us! From the Bible we draw all of our examples. It's a source of energy! The Bible isn't just about the past, it's happening today. If we place the Bible in our reality, we see that the power of Jesus' time is like our state today—and Pharaoh isn't that different from our large landowners!

"Prayer is so important. Prayer strengthens the spirit. But we can't leave aside faith and action. Our word for prayer is *oração,* which means *ora* (to pray) and *ação* (action). You have to pray and participate. Prayer strengthens the spirit, but it has to flow into action. I really believe God listens to our prayers. But we can't wait for answers to fall from heaven."

Participating in a grassroots Christian community is what brings prayer, Bible study, and action together. "It has changed my life," Antoinha says. "Belonging to a base community is a way to be a part of the Christian family."

Antoinha has trouble understanding both social activists who aren't rooted in faith and Christians who don't work actively for social change. "There are a lot of people in grass-roots work who aren't based in faith," she says. "Their labor doesn't yield fruit. It is like a seed that falls in gravel. As soon as the plant is born, it withers up. It doesn't have the inner force to go on. Our work always has its ups and downs, but we find strength as the community works in faith."

However, many Christians aren't bearing fruit either. "There are many people who use the Bible only for private prayer and don't see the action that's implicit in it. If you read, read, read, but don't do anything, what is essential to the Bible remains dead. Scripture is like a light for us. What is a light for? A light serves to illuminate our journey. If you just sit and stare at the light, you'll ruin your eyesight!"

Still, Antoinha encourages rather than criticizes. "I don't want to condemn people who don't have faith, nor people who aren't committed to our struggle. I don't want to condemn the rich—not at all! . . . I just hope they [the rich] begin to read a chapter, even a verse of the Bible, and begin to compare it with what's going on in society. This is the only way for them to understand the struggle. I'd just like people to pay attention to their own journey, step by step. Then they'll find the true reason to engage in the struggle to transform society."

Antoinha is confident that even those in different settings can follow this journey of conversion. It will take courage, she says, and therefore faith. It may be uncomfortable to look at the world as it really is. But everyone has some place to begin, she implies, if only they'll "stop and think a bit. Through their own life struggles, they'll find the need."

Are We Thirsty Enough?

Susan Classen is a nurse from Ohio. She works in El Salvador, training local health promoters in communities isolated by social neglect and the nation's ten-year civil war. She tells of walking one day from one village to another down a sun-baked road.

Sweat was dripping off Susan's forehead and running down her glasses as she walked up and down the hills. Her arms glistened with sweat. Her head pounded. As thirst set in, her mouth grew parched and dry. Water would be waiting in the next town—thirty minutes and "one more long haul uphill" away. With a desire to quench her thirst driving her forward, a thought crossed Susan's mind: "Does thirst for righteousness drive me the way physical thirst is driving me now?"

As Susan entered the town she ran into a friend carrying a bottle of warm, strawberry soda. Susan recalls: "She offered it to me and I drank with gusto. At the moment nothing mattered except the liquid sliding down my throat. We exchanged small talk and parted ways. I felt a new surge of energy."

Then another thought struck: "I hate strawberry soda." Susan especially hates it when it is warm. "Under normal circumstances I would have politely refused. I would have waited until I had other options for quenching my thirst."

She wonders: "Is that what I do with the gospel when a desperate thirst for righteousness is *not* driving me? Do I pick the parts of the gospel that make me feel good and leave what I don't like?" Susan notes that many North Americans tend to blame God for abandoning them if they experience difficulties, while poor Salvadorans sense God's presence in their suffering. Are North Americans simply not thirsty enough?

Susan recalls the story of a friend named Angélica, a young widow. Angélica had fled the fighting and repression in El Salvador for neighboring Honduras. After eight years, a longing for her home brought her back, despite continuing violence. She has seen violence of the most brutal sort.

When Angélica fled El Salvador, she was with a group of about a thousand others, mostly women and children. As they crossed the Sumpul River, which divides El Salvador and Honduras, the armies of the two nations closed in on each bank to cut off their escape. Soldiers massacred over six hundred of the fleeing refugees, including babies, and including Angélica's husband. She watched a hovering helicopter

cut him down with machine-gun fire. But she could not stop.
By swimming underwater, she escaped downstream.

When Susan heard Angélica's story, she asked, "Did you
ever get angry at God for letting this happen to you?" Angélica did not understand the question.

So Susan tried again: "If God is a good God, how could he
let you suffer so much?" Angélica still didn't know what Susan was asking.

Finally Susan turned the question around: "Did you feel
God's presence when you were fleeing?" Angélica's face lit
up. "Absolutely!" exclaimed the widow. "If it weren't for
God's presence with me, I wouldn't be here today."

Looking back on the conversation, Susan believes her
friend did not understand the first questions because they implied that life should be easy. "Too often our own theology
sees suffering as the result of sin in someone's life. If I can't
see that I've done anything to deserve the problems I encounter, I get mad at God for being unfair."

Susan wonders where North American Christians get that
idea. She notes that the apostle Paul certainly did not make
the Christian life sound easy. "We are hard pressed on every
side . . . perplexed . . . persecuted . . . struck down" (2 Corinthians 4:8-9). Yet Paul committed himself through "troubles,
hardships and distresses; in beatings, imprisonments and riots; in hard work, sleepless nights and hunger" (6:4-5).

"We first-world Christians are seldom desperate enough for
warm strawberry soda to quench our thirst," observes Susan.
"We want God to give us thirst quenchers that are ice-cold,
attractively packaged, and in a variety of flavors to suit our
every whim. Taking survival for granted, we try to make life
as easy and comfortable as possible. We concentrate on Bible
passages that fit a worldly definition of success. God seems to
fit right in with rich TV evangelists, multimillion-dollar Christian enterprises, and luxurious churches.

"When we read about the heroes of faith in Hebrews 11,
we want to be like those who 'shut the mouths of lions,
quenched the fury of the flames, and escaped the edge of the
sword.' But too often we ignore those who 'were stoned . . .

sawed in two . . . put to death by the sword.' Who wants heroes who 'went about in sheepskins and goatskins; destitute, persecuted and mistreated'? We unconsciously filter out passages that disturb our ideal of the easy Christian life.

"Poor, third-world Christians know life is hard. Reading the Bible, they identify with the many examples of God's presence among suffering people. They find comfort in the same passages that make us uncomfortable, that remind us to expect suffering. The poor don't need to pick and choose amid the daily struggle for survival. A desperate thirst drives third-world Christians toward a God who understands their pain.

"When I am really thirsty for righteousness, I welcome God in whatever way he chooses to reveal himself—in the good and the bad. When I am really thirsty, even warm strawberry soda tastes good."

Cycle of Faith and Action

Read the Bible. Read our world. Relate the two. Respond.

The grassroots Christian communities thriving throughout Latin America are living testimony to the power of connecting what we read in the Bible with what we read in our world. From Brazil, Antoinha reminds us to release this power by integrating faith and action, or responding. Susan Classen's testimony suggests that those of us who are not close to the world's need may have trouble reading the world and the Bible in a way that does justice to both.

Yet Susan's own example is helpful. Only a few of us will follow her to places like rural El Salvador. But if we can develop relationships with poor people, perhaps we can sense their needs as our own. Perhaps we can learn to read both Bible and world through their eyes. Perhaps we too can rediscover the power of the gospel.

Throughout these chapters, I am providing opportunities for you to do this. My hope is that if you aren't yet relating personally to people who are poor, then their stories and words in this book will supply the next best way of sensing a personal link. As we have studied the Bible, I have invited you to put yourself in their shoes and reread the Bible from the perspective of their worlds. Once again, with Susan's help, here is another story.

"I met Victorina, a poor Salvadoran, because she, along with 16 percent of her neighbors in a refugee camp, had tuberculosis. All four of her children died in infancy. She is illiterate and earns only enough money working full time to buy two pounds of beans a week.

"Victorina knows her place in society. She is last. She expects well-dressed people to move ahead of her in line at the doctor's office. She would not be surprised if the doctor told her, as he told her friend Marta, to 'stop wasting my time' because he had more important things to do than examine a 'dirty Indian.' Lacking dignity and confidence, Victorina would agree with the peasant man who told me, 'The poor are like disobedient children who deserve to be punished.' "

When poor people read the New Testament, they see a Jesus who treated poor people with patience and compassion, and who confronted and challenged the rich, notes Susan. Verses throughout the Bible that middle-class North Americans skim over will come alive for Victorina.

Imagine that you are Victorina. For the first time in your life you hear Psalm 12:5: " 'Because of the oppression of the weak and the groaning of the needy, I will now arise,' says the Lord, 'I will protect them from those who malign them.' " How would you feel?

Now, still imagining that you are Victorina, describe your reaction when you first hear Old Testament challenges to the powerful, such as the one in Isaiah 3:15: " 'What do you mean by crushing my people and grinding the faces of the poor?' declares the Lord."

Reassurance of God's love and active concern for poor people is foundational wherever the poor begin working together to transform their worlds, their society, and the conditions it has inflicted upon them. But rereading the Bible is not just a subjective, comforting experience. Reading and responding are in dynamic relationship.

A Chinese proverb goes something like this: "Unless I act on what I know, I don't know even that." We may never be fully able to put ourselves in the shoes of someone like Antoinha or Victorina. But at least we can learn this lesson from the poor who have discovered a renewed faith and a new way of reading the Bible in grassroots Christian communities: Unless we act on what we read in the Bible, we haven't yet learned to read.

If we do obey, we will continue to approach the Bible with fresh eyes. Acting on God's word leads to further reflection, which leads to further action. Susan recalls: "Four peasant health promoters in a Salvadoran village complained that their small clinic could not open until it had a table and shelves. They had already put their prayer and commitment into practice by volunteering to help meet the health needs of their community. They had come together to evaluate their experience and reflect on God's Word. But they felt community leaders were not supporting their efforts.

"We called a community meeting to see what could be done. The promoters explained the lack of support they felt and read the passage in 1 Peter 2:4-5 about building a spiritual temple with living stones. Lively discussion about what it means to be a community followed. By the end of the meeting, one man had donated a tree, four men agreed to chop it down and saw it into boards, three others volunteered to make a table and shelves, and four women formed a committee to organize fund-raising efforts."

So the cycle continues. Instead of the cycle of poverty and injustice, a cycle of faith, action, and dignity.

• • •

Learning by Heart

Read Luke 10:25-37; then reread verse 30.

Martin Luther King, Jr., wrote: "We are called to play the good Samaritan on life's roadside; but that will only be an initial act. One day we must see that the whole Jericho road must be transformed so that men and women will not be constantly beaten and robbed as they make their journey on life's highway."[1]

To transform the Jericho road, one must have some idea why there are robbers along it in the first place. Jesus does not say. What do you think?

A doctor told Victorina's friend to stop wasting his time because he had more important things to do than examine a "dirty Indian." If he read Luke 10, what reasons might he give for robbers on the Jericho road? What would Antoinha or Victorina say were the cause of robbers on the road?

●   ●   ●

For Thought and Discussion

1. Antoinha, a Brazilian Christian, says: "Scripture is like a light for us. What is a light for? A light serves to illuminate our journey. If you just sit and stare at the light, you'll ruin your eyesight!"

Have you ever read a familiar Scripture and caught your mind wandering elsewhere even as you read? Have you ever read a Scripture and discovered practical guidance for your life? What made the difference? And how would you feel about that text now if you had not acted on that guidance?

2. Recall the kind of Bible study that grassroots Christian communities in Brazil practice: *reading the Bible, reading the world, relating the two, responding.* Now think of Sunday school classes or Bible studies that you have been a part of. How have these methods of Bible study been similar? How have they been different?

3. Have poor people ever helped you understand the Bible better? Explain.

4. An African proverb says: "Until the lions have their historians, tales of hunting will always glorify the hunter." How will the church tend to interpret the Bible if poor people are not part of the discussion?

Note

1. Martin Luther King, Jr., *Beyond Vietnam and Casualties of the War in Vietnam* (New York: Clergy and Laity Concerned, 1985), p. 15.

9

Who Is the Neighbor?

WHAT DOES IT mean to be saved?

It may seem strange to ask such a question in a book like this. After all, if you, your friends, and I were not already gathered together as Christians around the Bible, we would not have gotten this far. With Paul, we are those who "know that our old self was crucified with [Christ] so that . . . we should no longer be slaves to sin" (Romans 6:6).

So getting saved from this bondage to sin and self is one thing. Each of us took care of that long ago, right? Now we have been studying what the Bible tells us about the poor. And that is another thing, right?

Sorry! If we are freed from slavery to sin and self, we are also freed to live for others. These are two sides of one coin. Everyone has many "others": those of other races, other nations, other cultures, other parts of town, other religious beliefs, other political ideologies, and those who are so other that we call them enemies. But North American middle-class life conspires to keep poor people out of sight and out of mind. Those of us who are not poor so easily accept this distance as natural and safe. Therefore, poor people are our others in a uniquely important way.

I am convinced that our relationship to people who are

poor is basic to life in Christ. If we have no such relationship, we had better ask ourselves once more what it means to be saved.

I realize that to speak of salvation and poverty in one breath is controversial. Christians have always debated the relationship between salvation and good works. Some see a debate between Paul and James in the very pages of the New Testament. Ever since Martin Luther took his unyielding stand for salvation "by faith alone," many Christians have felt that to stand anywhere but with Luther would risk sliding down a sandy bank. Taking a stand on social issues, or even talking too much about them, would lead into the salvation-by-good-works trap. Yet Jesus told us long ago that to endlessly debate this matter is to miss the whole point!

Skeptical? Are you already reaching for a concordance? Try looking up *scribe* or *lawyer*. Those fellows could argue until they had split all the hairs on your head—at least until they met Jesus. Your concordance will take you back to Luke 10:25 one more time, where a lawyer asked Jesus a question much like the one that begins this chapter: "What must I do to inherit eternal life?"

It's not that the lawyer thought he really needed to know. Actually, he "stood up to test Jesus." So Jesus turned the question around, asking him how he read the law of Moses. The lawyer replied that we are to love God with all our heart, soul, strength, and mind, and to love our neighbors as ourselves. "Do this," agreed Jesus, "and you will live."

But that was too obvious. The lawyer wanted a debate. If he kept splitting hairs, he could avoid facing his failure to meet his own standard. If he kept debating eternal life, he could put off actually living that life in loving relation to God and neighbor. And all the while he would be showing how much he, God's defender, cared about God's Word. So he asked Jesus, "Okay, just who is my neighbor?"

Luke takes care to note that the lawyer really "wanted to justify himself." Luther and like-minded Christians have been right to insist that we can't justify ourselves. It's no use trying to earn salvation by helping people who are poor. If that's what motivates any of us, we're still in bondage to self. We're still ultimately concerned more about our own destiny and needs than those of the poor.

But if we have to debate who our neighbors are—where our responsibility starts and stops—we are probably trying to justify ourselves too. If we are freed from slavery to self, we don't have to ask which others we owe love to. The louder some Christians insist on "justification by faith alone" while keeping a distance from the poor, the more I have to wonder if they are still trying to do the justifying themselves after all.

Justification *is* by God's grace. Conversion to our others is by God's grace. Christlike letting go of self is only possible in and through Christ. After all, the more we try to forget ourselves, the deeper into self-fixation we sink. It's like when I was eight years old and lay awake trying to forget the tune of a cigarette commercial. I thought I was sinning just to have it in my head. But the more I tried to forget it, the more it obsessed me!

I am aware that I can't make conversion happen to you. In fact, *you* can't make it happen to you. We need God's loving touch of grace. What I can do is tell you about someone who has felt that touch, someone who can't help reaching out to touch others. And I can pray that God will take her story deep into your soul like an acupuncture needle, touching a nerve and deadening the tiresome pain of endless self-worry.

"God Gave Me a Gift—and I Love"

Kris Hill lives in a small, drafty house in inner-city Denver. Like the outcast Samaritan who stopped to aid a robbery victim on the Jericho road, she has lived all her life at the margin of society. She is an Afro-American woman, and now she is old. She is all but illiterate. But as she likes to point out, "It don't take education to serve God. Uneducated—can't hardly read my name—but you'd be surprised the things that I really know. They came from God. Nobody else taught me." Kris Hill knows what it's like at the margin.

"I was so embarrassed day before yesterday to stand up

there in the line to get cheese. No butter—they were supposed to give me butter and flour and stuff like that. But I didn't take the flour because I had some left over, and it would just waste because I don't know how to use that. I took the cheese because my grandson uses the cheese. But I was so embarrassed. That's the first time that ever happened to me; because when I was a young woman, I worked for my living. I didn't make much, but I worked for my living. When you get older, that's the kind of thing that can happen to you. It pulls you down.

"So I said, 'The TV people need to be out to see this. Now that's a sight to see. People in line waiting to get a little cheese and a little butter, a pound of butter, and flour or cornmeal. Now that looks bad for this country. With all the rich people, that looks real bad.' "

Kris Hill shares more with the Samaritan, however. She too is neighborly. She is literally creating a hospitable space for those who are even needier than herself. It takes all her stubborn persistence to get help out of the city's urban renewal program, but she is slowly trying to fix up her house for this purpose.

"A lot of the church people are living in luxury. And the world—them that's out there that don't have—they see it too. See, people may be down and out; but they know if you love them or not. They have feelin's too. What I say to the church world is, 'We should get off these beautiful pews and go out there and get some of these people and bring 'em in.' "

And that's what she does—brings others in, sits them down on her praying chair, and sits them down in her kitchen for beans. Simple actions for a simple reason: she has experienced God's love and wants to share that love with others.

"If it wasn't for God, I couldn't do this, what I'm doin'. See, I pray and talk to God about it. That's the only way I can make it. If it wasn't for God, I couldn't do anything, even in my past. Because I was so poor, there have been times I thought, I'll just go down there to the Mississippi River and jump in. But something would always come to keep me from just takin' off. I had the three little children, and I didn't want to leave my children. That was my life. They were my life. They kept me going. But when God came into my life, it changed everything.

"There are a lot of people who want to be changed, but people won't go and get 'em. He says for us to go and bring them in. He says, 'You go out.' Like if I go down the street today and meet someone that is down and out in spirit, I talk with them and say, 'Why don't you come and go home with me and let me pray for you?' They may be hungry. Maybe I have some beans to give 'em. You feed 'em; then you pray for 'em. You pray for 'em; then you feed 'em. Either one—whatever comes first.

"So if I meet someone who is down and out and they want to come and let me pray for them and help them—that's what God wants me to do. I know what it means to be outside with no place to live and someone takes me in. I know about that. And when I pass and look at these people layin' on the ground, it hurts me so bad, because they need help. Somebody needs to go and get them. We have shelters, but we need more shelters.

"God gave me a gift when he saved me—and I love. That's one of the main things—I love. I don't care how nasty or bad they look; I love. God put that in me, that love. I don't care what they look like. No color. They're human beings; they look like me. But they need my help. And that's what I'm gonna do. That's what it's all about. And I have to obey that. I don't know how long it's gonna take. I need help to straighten this place out, but there is gonna be some help. I'm gonna do it by the help of God.

"See that red chair? That's what that's for. So far I've got different ones comin' here, and they know what the chair is for. And they go there and pray. I told a little boy who came, 'You know you are blessed to make it into this house in this neighborhood? You thank God for making it from the sidewalk into this house. Because somebody could have been shootin' at somebody else and you'd got it.' He said, 'Yes, ma'am, that's right.' I said, 'Go there to that altar there and thank God for your life.' And he did.

"It's workin'. It's gonna work. It's gonna be better as soon as I get the house really fixed up like I want to. I want some of the poor to come and eat here, eat some beans and bread. That's what it's all about. It's no use for me to live here if I can't do this, because it's on my heart and I obeys my heart. It may seem strange and funny to other people, but I've got to do what my heart says. It's gonna work out. It won't be glamorous, but it's gonna work out."

The Samaritan's Mercy

Those who are neighborly don't have to ask the lawyerly question, "Please, sir, exactly who is this alleged neighbor of mine?" That is Jesus' message, as he deftly turns the question around.

But how do we "go and do likewise"? It's possible to go through the motions—give handouts, make a show of charity —and end up feeding our own selfish egos at least as much as we feed the poor. How shall we go and likewise become neighborly? Is it possible to become so self-forgetting that neighborliness, even when inconvenient, becomes entirely natural?

Probably not. Our fallen human condition, our twisted self-concern, is too pervasive. Denying ourselves, *by ourselves,* is like trying to suppress an unwanted tune. Only another richer and livelier song will drive it out.

What is possible is to look our needy condition squarely in the eye, with no attempt to justify either ourselves or our nettlesome selfishness. What is possible is to freely admit our own need and see ourselves in the light of God's love. What is possible is to listen for that new song.

We know more about who the Samaritan was, and what he did, than we know about his motives. As a Samaritan, whom the Jews despised, he did not have to worry about preserving his reputation. In contrast, the priest and Levite who passed by would not have wanted to soil their ritual cleanliness or be late for their official appointments. But the Samaritan was already at the margin.

As Joyce, from the Welcome Inn church in Hamilton, Ontario, told us in chapter 3, "Somehow our coverings have been taken off [through poverty and troubled backgrounds]. We've been brought down to a point where the things that really matter are all that's left—your dignity, your love for people around you, your love for God, and his love for you."

Of the Samaritan, Jesus says simply that he had compassion. The lawyer recognizes that he showed mercy. This is a clue. Throughout the Gospels, Jesus consistently links God's mercy toward us with the mercy we show others. In the Beatitudes we learn, "Blessed are the merciful, for they will be shown mercy" (Matthew 5:7; Luke 6:36). In the Lord's Prayer we pray, "Forgive us our debts, as we also have forgiven our debtors" (Matthew 6:12; Luke 11:4).

If this seems like earning God's mercy or forgiveness, things can move the other way too. In Luke 7, while Jesus is dining at the house of Simon the Pharisee, a prostitute comes and anoints Jesus' feet. When Simon takes offense, Jesus tells him, "Her many sins have been forgiven—for she loved much. But he who has been forgiven little loves little" (Luke 7:47).

To love much, to freely show mercy, to instinctively sense compassion, to serve our others, to turn toward those who are poor—for this we desperately need to remember just how much mercy God has shown us. Throughout the entire Bible, this is the pattern. "We love because [God] first loved us" (1 John 4:19).

The poor, oppressed, and needy are not a *should,* even in what we call the law of Moses. They are a *therefore,* a natural response to God's love. Exodus 22:21-22 (RSV) puts it this way: "You shall not wrong a stranger or oppress him, for you were strangers in the land of Egypt [until the Lord mercifully saved you]. You shall not afflict any widow or orphan." This pattern was at the heart of Israel's worship experience (see Deuteronomy 26:1-15).

We too have been victims. Perhaps the robbers in the hill country east of Jerusalem, landless or unemployed, with hungry mouths at home driving them to crime, were victims. Even the priest and Levite, trapped in religious systems that snuffed out their hearts' warm flame of love for God and neighbor, were victims too.

How, then, do we "go and do likewise" with simplicity and compassion? How do we let mercy mold our hearts? By remembering the immense love God has shown us.

That Gratitude May Convert Us

In the early chapters of this book, we discovered that in ways we sometimes fear to admit, the poor are us. We also heard testimonies of personal renewal and church renewal through relationships with poor people. As we began to study the Bible from the vantage point of the poor, we learned to recognize some of the *highways* that society creates to keep us from the poor. Though such highways crisscross the face of the earth, we peeked at God's vision for a new earth and new heavens—a new creation where no one goes hungry, for no one labors, plants, or builds in vain.

Fortunately, this new order, the kingdom of God, is breaking into human affairs already. Jesus offers the good news that we can begin even now to reorient our lives according to kingdom values. In chapter 7, we reminded ourselves that poor people must be active participants in this kingdom, not its passive recipients. In fact, they, like the formerly blind man before the Sanhedrin, are the ones who are asking us if *we* will participate too.

Now, as we struggle to answer yes to this invitation, we dig down deep for resources. At first we may find only selfishness, self-justification, the inability to forget our own needs and think of others. But then we discover that recognizing neediness, which we can never fill alone, opens us to God and to our neighbors. We need both. The commandment to love our neighbors is like the commandment to love God. God has loved us fully and indiscriminately. A desire to respond "likewise" sprouts in our hearts.

This desire is like a tulip in the winter snow. God planted the tulip bulb of love long ago, at creation. But for too long it has lain dormant. With the promise of spring, the promise of a new beginning, of a new heavens and a new earth, of a new season of God's sunshine, it pushes through our thawing hearts and cold exterior. To love our others, those who are poor, may begin to be an instinctive response to God's love after all—as it was for the Samaritan; as it is for Kris Hill.

• • •

Learning by Heart

Read Luke 10:25-37.

The lawyer finally had to admit that the question of who is the neighbor had nothing to do with which needy ones were deserving. One of those he surely thought undeserving provided the model of neighborliness. A despised Samaritan was "the one who had mercy." What is this model of love and mercy? Who is this neighbor? Are we neighborly, as this one was?

It cost the Samaritan something to love. What costs might we need to bear? What privilege might we need to give up? What "inconvenience" might we need to take on?

The Samaritan loved without any prospect that the roadside victim would return that love or even express gratitude. What determines our willingness to become the neighbor? Do we love, expecting something in return? If so, have we really loved?

The Samaritan's commitment to the other was open-ended and ongoing. How far are we willing to go in becoming the neighbor? Have we already placed limits on how far we will go in relation to those who are poor? What might those limits be?

• • •

For Thought and Discussion

1. Read the following Scriptures: Exodus 22:21-27; Deuteronomy 26:5-13; Matthew 5:43-48; 1 John 2:7-11; 4:7-12, 19-21. What is the link between love of God and love of neighbor?

2. What are some disguised ways that people ask: And who

is my neighbor? What are some specific ways that someone who is truly saved is freed to live for others?

3. Read Matthew 18:23-34, a parable about forgiveness and mercy. Then prayerfully respond to each of the following questions:

- In what ways am I poor, needy, or a victim? How has God shown love for me in my need, canceled my debts, or given me opportunities to begin anew?

- Have I been ungrateful? If so, how? Has a lack of grateful love toward God expressed itself in callousness toward my needy neighbor in the world today? How?

- Have I imprisoned myself in loneliness and selfishness, prejudice or materialism? How?

- Who are my others? How will I express fresh gratitude to God through renewed compassion toward them?

10

What Shall We Do?

IN CHAPTER 2, we looked at how the *breakdown of community, centralization of power,* and *individualistic choices* are impoverishing not only poor people but the nonpoor as well.

Wherever people begin to organize at the grassroots, however, they have a chance to rebuild bonds of community. Wherever they rebuild community, they take back some of the power they have lost to distant government bureaucracies and impersonal corporations. Wherever they do these things to look out, not only for their own interests, but also for the interests of others (Philippians 2:4), they begin trading in individualistic ways and seeking the common good of all who share our beleaguered planet.

And if nothing else, they retain hope and replenish energy. Author and radio talk-show host Studs Terkel notes: "The great overwhelming many of us sit by and feel rather pessimistic. But the people who are actually active in something in the community or in the country, who actually express opinions and are fervent about it, have a little more hope than those who sit by, those who are just accepting. In fact, they have considerably more than a little more hope. So maybe there's a little moral there somewhere."

For people to become part of the solution to poverty, rather than part of the problem, many and diverse things must happen. But wherever one sees hopeful signs of people making a difference, chances are that they are doing three things. They are *starting locally, making global connections,* and *working with others* through grassroots communities and wider networks joining them together. This, then, is our task. This is our hope.

Keep Listening

As Valerie Werner discusses community organizing, she makes some comparisons that are not complimentary to the church. But, then, sometimes "Samaritans" do a better job at what God's people should be doing than the church itself. Just as the lawyer needed to learn from one whose religious and racial mixture offended him, so may we. Often we may need to humbly observe and join their efforts as a way to rediscover our own calling as followers of Jesus. Discovering those efforts and resisting the temptation to duplicate or compete with them can be the first step in beginning to work locally.

Valerie has been part of tenant organizations in Illinois and Indiana. She grew up poor and married as a teenager. Later, as a single mother of three living in the sprawling public housing projects of southside Chicago, such cooperation was a matter of survival.

Tenant organizations in cities like St. Louis, Washington, D.C., and Chicago have developed a system of self-management. Instead of waiting for the Department of Housing and Urban Development to do repairs, for example, they contract with the government to do their own repairs. Sometimes they even hire and train convicted vandals to help them qualify to move back into an apartment. When a tenant organization manages its own apartment block, it may dedicate a few of the spaces to community services, such as a community kitchen, after-school programs for children, and day-care. Not only are tenant-run services more convenient; they also keep resources and employment in the community.

When Valerie began to get out of poverty and attend college, she gave back some of the community support she had received from fellow tenants in Chicago by helping organize a tenants' organization in the college town. The way to begin was something we will recognize by now. It is listening to people's stories.

"We are talking grassroots—women who come together and share food stamps so they can buy large quantities of food and save money. It starts with networking like that. If you keep them isolated, then they don't do anything. If you get them together to tell their stories and then somebody says, 'We can do something about this,' that is when things happen. And that is how it happens in Chicago. It always comes from people organizing. I love that. That is where I experience spirit. That is where I feel the Spirit. Do you know what I mean?

"I don't feel the Spirit when I go to church; so I don't go to church anymore. I don't know what I feel about church. All these people go, but you don't know the person next to you really well. You are not crying together or bleeding together or sharing stories. And so I would rather go to tenants' meetings. We do those things there. And that is where my spirit gets fed. Sometimes we talk about God. Actually more and more we have been.

"See, the problem with church people is if they want to help, they want things done their way. That has been my experience. So they are not listening to the people saying, 'This is what we feel we need, and this is what we want.' A lot of times church people are more educated than the other ones. They come in and say, 'Well, I just know exactly what you need; let me help you.'

"How do you tell church people to go in and just listen and help [people] create the communities that they want to create? Allow people that kind of freedom to create what they feel is best for them. Listen to their ideas. You are not struggling with the same things and you don't feel the same fears.

"I think there is something to be learned by being vulnerable that way. You learn something about life that you never learn if you are never vulnerable. You start to realize just how dependent you are, that you really need other people. I really need other people in my life in order to make my life work. I don't have a bank account to fall back on and I don't have a permanent home and I need people to help me with my children sometimes. So I have to ask people to help me. But I think part of being human is realizing that we do need each other.

"I do know some people—these are individuals, but I am sure that churches could do this—who provide funds for inner-city development programs without providing opinions. If there is a Lutheran church in a low-income area and the people inside the church are also involved in the community, wouldn't it be good if a Lutheran church in the suburbs could send funding into this church, no strings attached? They could fund housing programs, educational workshop programs, and things like that.

"I don't think the poor want them to come in on Sunday and go. If they want to do so something significant, then they need to move there and let their children play with the children in the neighborhoods and go to the same schools and be a part of the community. If they are not willing to be a part of the community then they should leave us alone. . . .

"The funny thing is that I miss those neighborhoods in Chicago. We used to sit out on the porches and yell from each other's windows and watch each other's kids; and there is a lot of stuff that goes on in those neighborhoods that gives it a richness. It doesn't happen in the suburbs. People become so distant from one another.

"I would think that if you are going to work in the community, [it would be good] to do some research before you even get there to find out what is going on, who is *grassrootsing* it, if that is the kind of work you want to do. Meet the people before you come to live with them. Listen to their stories. Don't you love people's stories? I love to listen to people's stories. That is what I would do."

Begin Locally, Connect Globally, Work Together

One priest who has not bypassed the needy who have confronted him on the way is Dom Hélder Câmara. For many years, Dom Hélder was an archbishop in Recife, Brazil. For the poor of that city, he was an especially beloved shepherd. But for many others, in many other countries, for many years, Dom Hélder has been a winsome Latin American apostle of nonviolent social change on behalf of the world's poor. His counsel helps us outline our tasks: begin locally, work outward toward global issues, and work together.

● *Begin locally.* "We must repeat and underscore this truth," Dom Hélder says. "In order to feel the world's injustices as if they were our own, the best path is to set out from local injustices." To understand rural poverty in the underdeveloped regions of the third world, he suggests studying the neglected rural areas of one's own country. To make the connections between unemployment, migrant labor, and the hoarding of technology both at home and abroad, he insists learning about your own regional economy.

The task is as close to home as our own life. "Since we must obtain justice as a condition of peace, may each one begin by examining whether one is at peace with justice or whether one is committing injustices." But don't stop at the personal level either. Work with "the neighbors, the *barrio,* the community until reaching brothers and sisters of all races, all tongues, and all religions."

● *Connect local and global.* Dom Hélder has chided do-gooders and protesters alike for not developing a global vision. Their activities may be generous and well-intended. But they have not always taken into account the economic, cultural, and political structures that create local problems. Even those who protest hunger, war, and human rights abuses in the third world may not reach deeply enough if they only address isolated cases. "We will work in vain for changes in the structures of oppression in poor countries if we do not carry out the same effort in the industrialized nations."

The struggle for justice is "the great tidal wave of our time." We must shrug off the accusations of those in power.

"Without justice there will be no peace. There are grave injustices in the poor countries. There are grave injustices in the rich countries. And there are extremely grave injustices in the relations between the rich and the poor countries."

Dom Hélder notes that even if the developed nations double or triple their level of foreign aid for underdeveloped nations, it will not be enough unless they also revise international trade, banking, and debt policy. "It is not enough to do philanthropy and send a few crumbs to the miserable ones in the third world. Often government aid to poor countries is nothing more than palliatives to hide the justice denied them by international trade policies."

- *Work together.* Yet even in the face of such global challenges, Dom Hélder comes back again and again to the power of small local initiatives. Wherever people begin, in whatever city or nation, race or religion, they become "Abrahamic minorities," however small their efforts. Their bond is that they join with Father Abraham to "hope against all hope." And their power is that they join together, first in small groups and then in networks between small groups.

This is the step that makes all the others possible. "As forerunner and sign of the profound changes that must be achieved at the national, continental, and global levels, we need something more than the force of an idea. We need a touch of grace, an impulse from on high." That touch comes when we gather together, "for where two or three come together in my name," says Jesus, "there am I with them."

And what about our Samaritans—non-Christians working for change? We need them too. We need them especially. As Dom Hélder trusts, "We are and we will be with Christ—even though we may not know it and even though we apparently do not want it—to the degree that our hunger and thirst for justice, truth, and love is sincere."

The Touch of Grace When We Gather

As Dom Hélder reminds us, handouts can be a substitute for justice. But awareness of social issues, even all the right rhetoric about the need for social justice, can also be a substitute for acting.

To spur and sustain action, we need abiding relationships. We need ongoing relationships with people who are poor. We need ongoing relationships with fellow Christians who are concerned about the poor. And wherever possible, we need circles that bring both together—places where we all may share our poverty and our wealth.

Jesus once told the story of a father and two brothers. The father asked them to work in his vineyard. The first said he wouldn't, but then changed his mind and went. The second said he would, but never got around to it (Matthew 21:28-32). Frankly, I worry about some of my socially aware friends. Their hearts seem to be in the right places. At least they say the right things about the right issues. But they aren't much more involved in the lives of poor people than they would be if they thought social issues had no place in church.

In fact, I would be more optimistic if they went door-to-door handing out tracts or delivering Christmas baskets in inner cities and rural hollers. Such actions would bring them into personal contact with the poor. Some of the most zealous advocates for social justice are Christians who began by seeking to save *souls.* Then they discovered that they could not isolate soul from body. They remembered that bodies live in societies. They learned more about how societies work politically. They got involved. Yet they have never cut themselves off from the moorings and nourishment of their spiritual roots.

I have seen at least three things happen to socially aware friends. Sometimes their social concern is mostly the product of a certain kind of education. There's nothing wrong with that, except that now their education and their professional status keep them from developing personal relationships with poor people.

Sometimes they have begun with grassroots work among the poor and then learned more and more about the wider social, economic, and political causes of poverty. Unfortunately, they have also allowed their work on *issues* to move them off the street altogether and behind desks.

Or sometimes, they have simply burned out in the face of so much human need. Before they quite realized it, their well of love had gone dry. "We love because [God] first loved us," says 1 John 4:19. Suddenly they were experiencing neither God's love nor their own.

I sympathize because all these things have happened to me at one time or another. They have happened when I have lost touch with either my friends in the church among the poor or my friends in the church among the nonpoor. Both groups have resources, a wealth to fill the poverty of the other. I too need those resources, those relationships, to stay empowered and hopeful.

All of us need the "touch of grace from on high" that comes when we gather together in grassroots Christian communities, as my friends in the church among the poor so often find they must do. And I don't mean ingrown ethnic communities or suburban encounter groups. Those are usually closed circles. I mean outward-looking, inviting circles—circles of mission, service, and relationship to our others, people who are poor.

Our North American churches among the nonpoor do have much to share. Yes, we must continue to learn how to share without demeaning poor people. But, we have resources that few people, now or in history, could begin to imagine. We have opportunities, personal choices, material goods, and capital. We have technological expertise, entrepreneurial finesse, and political clout. We have unparalleled freedom to form voluntary associations, citizens' lobbies, interest groups, and creative business enterprises. We have access to a wealth of learning from Christians throughout the ages and throughout our world today. Wisely and humanely managed, all these resources can serve God's kingdom and God's passion—the poor.

And yet we of all people are sometimes the most discouraged! "What can we do?" we ask, not really expecting an answer. Why? We are disconnected. Rich in so many resources, we ignore the one resource we need most—one another. Our fellow human beings. Poor people. Our brothers and sisters in

Christ. The kind of face-to-face relationships that are rooted in small, committed clusters of Christians, but that open out to others throughout our neighborhoods and throughout our world.

In many places poor people have few resources besides each other and little power except their numbers and organization. Yet because they must depend on each other, and on the Christ who makes his home among them, they are rich in faith and hope. Can we too create outward-looking grassroots Christian communities within our congregations? Our need to form such groups is less obvious to us than it is to the poor. But we need them at least as much.

I once observed a model for this kind of grassroots community building within middle-class North American churches at Hyattsville Mennonite Church near Washington, D.C. Many North American congregations have small groups, Bible studies, or discipleship groups to nurture Christian life in ways that are not possible on a Sunday morning. At Hyattsville they call these "covenant groups." But in 1982 a handful of members invited others to join them in forming a group that would both look inward and minister outward. Its focus was on Central America and Central American refugees in the Washington area.

It was the group's commitment to supporting each other in both the inward journey and an outward journey that made it unique. Journaling, prayer, and Bible study were part of the inward journey. Aiding refugee families, witnessing to government representatives, and political action were part of the outward journey. As the group learned from both the pain and the faith that Central Americans brought with them, its commitment to integrating faith and action deepened.

The group did not expect everyone in the congregation to be as knowledgeable or active in Central American issues as they. What they did ask of the whole congregation was support, blessing, prayer, and an open ear when particularly pressing needs arose. Those needs might be used furniture for a new family or letters to Congress at crucial moments. After a year of discussions, the church voted to declare itself a sanctuary to harbor refugees, whatever their legal status.

The Central America Covenant Group continued for five years. When it did disband, other outgrowths lived on. One couple accepted a term of voluntary service in Honduras. Two other members married and took an educational honeymoon in Central America. Two interchurch agencies for refugees that the group helped to begin continue in the Washington area.

No one group or congregation can take on every issue and human need that confronts them. But I dream of a cluster of people in each congregation making a persevering commitment to learn about one cause of poverty and respond to people who are poor. Together with the poor, these clusters could transform their congregations, their congregations might transform their towns and neighborhoods, and Christ's church might yet transform the face of the earth. It may be a dream, but I believe it is God's dream.

There is much work to do, but we can do many things. And we can do them joyfully, hopefully, and tirelessly. But we must work together.

I am confident that we will find what is ours to do in our locality, from our edge of the global challenge, if we really want to. To help you get started, part two of this book provides resources to help you begin "Making Connections" locally and beyond. It will give you a jump on things you could do anyway. You can research national and international organizations. You can explore existing local initiatives. You can discover needs few others are noticing. You can keep listening to the poor.

Expand your current circles. Form new circles. Meet people who are poor. Meet yourself and God in the poor. Form a continuing grassroots Christian community within your congregation. Discover together the actions that merge love of God and love of neighbor. Embrace good news among the poor. You are the neighbor.

•   •   •

Learning by Heart

Read Luke 10:25-37.

What would be the impact of this passage without the last sentence, in which Jesus tells the lawyer to "go and do likewise"? What will the impact of this study be on your life, your congregation, and your community if you, like the lawyer, do not "go and do likewise"?

> Almighty God, who created us in your own image: Grant us grace fearlessly to contend against evil and to make no peace with oppression; and, that we may reverently use our freedom, help us to employ it in the [building] of justice in our communities and among the nations, to the glory of your holy name; through Jesus Christ our Lord, who lives and reigns with you and the Holy Spirit, one God, now and for ever. *Amen.*[1]

• • •

For Thought, Discussion, and Action

1. Did you make and follow through on the commitment to seek out a face-to-face encounter with the poor in your local area? If not, skip ahead to question 2 below. If you have had a personal encounter with poor people, take some time to process your experience, even if you need an extra session:

• What were the high and low points of your experience? What made you feel compassion? What made you feel angry? What was hardest to accept?

• Explore the reasons for any internal struggle or conflict that the experience prompted within you. Why do you think you reacted as you did?

• What did you learn about poor people? What did you learn about how society works?

• Did you sense a compulsion to respond to poverty in new ways? Share any emerging sense of calling with others.

2. Asking yourself the following questions might move you toward responses to poverty and relationships with poor people that will be appropriate to your own context, concerns, and skills—or those of your group. If you cannot answer all the questions at once, that is fine. Note areas where you will

need to investigate, and jot down how and when you will do so. Part two of this book will provide further information, analysis, addresses, and resources to help you.

Responding locally

• Are there hungry people within ten miles of your home or church? How can you find out and get in contact?

• Identify two or three of the most pressing problems of poverty and injustice in your town, city, or region of the country. The problems may be close to home. Members of some rural congregations may suffer from the farm crisis. In urban congregations members may be affected by plant closures and unemployment.

• If the problems seem far away, what does that say about your congregation or lifestyle?

Connecting globally

• Identify two or three global problems of poverty and injustice, particularly ones whose causes have local dimensions. Some examples are arms industries in our communities, agribusinesses controlling more and more land both at home and abroad, personal lifestyle, and consumption.

• What are some local connections to these global problems?

• What are some global connections to the local problems you listed above?

• If you are not aware of any local-global connections, is that because there aren't any or because you need to learn more?

Working together

• What are the two or three problems, local or global, that most concern you or your group?

• Which of these are you in the best position to work on?

• Are there other people in the congregation or community who are already working on this issue? How can you learn from or join forces with them?

• Are there national organizations that could help you respond, organize, and do further research?

• How can your group organize itself (whether launching a new effort or joining another one) to sustain its mission over time through prayer, Bible study, and continued reflection on its activities for justice?

• If you are not part of a group already, ask yourself: Whom do I know who would share my concern for poor people and be interested in meeting regularly for mutual support and planning, for prayer and ongoing study?

Note

1. *The Book of Common Prayer* (Seabury; Winston Press facsimile edition, 1976), p. 260.

11

A Closing Prayer

Invocation

"Come, all you who are thirsty,
  come to the waters;
and you who have no money,
  come, buy and eat!
Come, buy wine and milk
  without money and without cost.
Why spend money on what is not bread,
  and your labor on what does not satisfy?
Listen, listen to me, and eat what is good,
  and your soul will delight in the richest of fare.
Give ear and come to me;
  hear me, that your soul may live" (Isaiah 55:1-3).

Lord God, Creator of all the earth, Sustainer of all life, we turn to call on you. We turn to ask, as your Son Jesus Christ taught us to do, for daily bread. We turn to ask it for ourselves and for the poor of all the world.

But, behold, it is you who have been calling! So often mouthing prayers of habit, rather than prayers of heart, we have been deaf to your ancient and abiding call. Hunger of soul and stomach has never been your doing. In all places you have offered good things to all creatures, making rain to fall on the just and the unjust. In all times you have offered drink to the thirsty and bread to the hungry.

Yet heedless of your call, we have hungered. Building our own kingdoms, rather than your kingdom, our greatest achievements prove hollow. Feasting on the earth's bounty apart from the poor, we grow fat and unhealthy yet never have enough. We labor, but in vain, when we do not labor justly.

O Lord, you know what it is that will truly satisfy. It is you, your ways, and your people that satisfy. For truly, to love you with all our heart, soul, strength, and mind, and to love neighbor as self are not burdensome commandments, but the grace and richness of life itself.

Merciful and patient God, speak once again and enable us to hear and to come so that our souls may live.

Confession

"Surely the arm of the Lord is not too short to save,
    nor his ear too dull to hear.
But your iniquities have separated you from your God;
your sins have hidden his face from you,
    so that he will not hear.
For your hands are stained with blood,
    your fingers with guilt.
Your lips have spoken lies,
    and your tongue mutters wicked things.
No one calls for justice;
    no one pleads his case with integrity.
They rely on empty arguments and speak lies;
    they conceive trouble and give birth to evil. . . .
The way of peace they do not know;
    there is no justice in their paths.
They have turned them into crooked roads;
    no one who walks in them will know peace.
So justice is far from us,
    and righteousness does not reach us.

We look for light, but all is darkness;
　for brightness, but we walk in deep shadows. . . .
For our offenses are many in your sight,
　and our sins testify against us.
Our offenses are ever with us,
　and we acknowledge our iniquities" (Isaiah 59:1-4, 8-9, 12).

We confess, holy God, that the words of the prophet too often apply to us. We have been indifferent to the cry of the poor. When we *have* paid attention, we have too often let bias and condescension control our attitudes. We have been disrespectful of their cultures, values, courage, and strength in adversity. We have seized upon hearsay and half-truths about the poor instead of listening to them. To justify our own neglect, we have found subtle ways to blame the victims of oppression for their own plight. Forgive us, Lord.

Sovereign God, even those of us who take pride in our concern for the poor sometimes find sophisticated ways to elude them. We demand just a little more information before we can act. We pretend that right opinions will take the place of right actions. We make merely token changes in lifestyle. We look down upon those with "less enlightened" views about social justice, while refusing to humble ourselves to live and work among the poor. We noisily protest injustices in South Africa, Poland, Latin America, and the Philippines. Yet we prosper from injustices closer to home. When our property values are the ones that might drop, we sell out in time. When our job or scholarship might provide another group with long-overdue opportunities, our prophetic voice grows strangely silent. Forgive us, Lord.

Proclamation

"Is not this the kind of fasting I have chosen:
to loose the chains of injustice
　and untie the cords of the yoke,
to set the oppressed free
　and break every yoke?

Is it not to share your food with the hungry
    and to provide the poor wanderer with shelter—
when you see the naked, to clothe him,
    and not to turn away from your own flesh and blood?
Then your light will break forth like the dawn,
    and your healing will quickly appear;
then your righteousness will go before you,
    and the glory of the Lord will be your rear guard.
Then you will call, and the Lord will answer;
    you will cry for help, and he will say: Here am I"
      (Isaiah 58:6-9).

Lord God, we stand amazed. What first seemed like bad news has turned out to be good news! Your fast, the work that loomed so discomforting, is our own healing. The dim path of unlearning old values bursts forth into a clearing of light. The glory of life in you has appeared where we least expected it. In the poor, we learn to know you anew. You are present most passionately in those places we readily avoid.

You have given us the opportunity for reconciliation with you our God and with our neighbors the poor. You are liberating us from false securities, from crafty idols that promise the peace and prosperity only you can give. You are freeing us to live authentic lives of integrity, justice, and right relations with humanity and the earth. You even offer this peerless adventure: to join in your kingdom beginning now, to participate as your movement breaks into human history.

Still, we have so much to learn from our Lord, Jesus of Nazareth, about being disciples. We have so much to learn from the poor about being hospitable friends. Sometimes we grow weary. Sometimes we despair. Grant us to hunger and thirst after justice, so that we may truly fast. Nourish us in your word, in worship, and in co-laboring with our sisters and brothers. Satiate us not, except in the fullness of your kingdom.

When we feast, may it be at a table set with the flavors of many tribes and nations, a table where all who likewise hunger for justice may feel welcome, a table that signs for your kingdom. Received by your grace, may we be a people of truly graceful hospitality toward other peoples. Fed at your table, may we live out your Eucharist in the world, letting our own lives be broken and shared for the healing of others.

When we fast, may we recognize the cords you would have us undo, the yokes you would have us break. Give us the courage to name oppression for what it is—the boldness to face pharaohs and Pharisees alike. Give us also the wit to notice those who long to put aside violent ways of exploitation and join your kingdom movement: Levi the tax collector, Zacchaeus the wealthy, and Cornelius the soldier of occupation.

Above all, grant us the gentleness to encourage the oppressed without breaking bruised reeds or snuffing out the hope that yet burns in the poor. Free us from all paternalism and condescension, from all need to be right or in charge. Remind us to cry to you for help, rather than to justify ourselves, so that in our need for your love, we may love others in their need.

Thanksgiving

"Listen to me, you who pursue righteousness
     and who seek the Lord:
Look to the rock from which you were cut
     and to the quarry from which you were hewn;
look to Abraham, your father,
     and to Sarah, who gave you birth.
When I called him he was but one,
     and I blessed him and made him many.
The Lord will surely comfort Zion
     and will look with compassion on all her ruins;
he will make her deserts like Eden,
     her wastelands like the garden of the Lord.
Joy and gladness will be found in her,
     thanksgiving and the sound of singing" (Isaiah 51:1-3).

We do thank you, Creator God, Messiah Jesus, Empowering Spirit. We thank you for the work of faith, hope, and blessing to all nations, which you began in Sarah and Abraham. We thank you for the work of liberating salvation, which you realized in Jesus Christ. We thank you that this work of calling, blessing, and liberation continues through your people today. Truly, it is the only foundation on which to build our lives.

But we thank you also for the poor, who have graciously opened their lives to us, who have told their stories, who have evangelized us and let us in on their secret—Christ among them!

Thank you for giving us the ability to listen and the power to respond. We are not trapped in golden cages of affluence! You rebuild the ruins of lives caught in poverty. You create oases of holy simplicity amid the desert of materialism. You restore the true prosperity of human fellowship and respect for the earth even though we have wasted the earth you gave us. You draw a new circle. You make us neighbors.

Covenant and Commission

"The Spirit of the Sovereign Lord is on me,
    because the Lord has anointed me
    to preach good news to the poor.
He has sent me to bind up the brokenhearted,
    to proclaim freedom for the captives
    and release from darkness for the prisoners,
to proclaim the year of the Lord's favor
    and the day of vengeance of our God,
to comfort all who mourn,
    and provide for those who grieve in Zion—
to bestow on them a crown of beauty
    instead of ashes,
the oil of gladness
    instead of mourning,
and a garment of praise
    instead of a spirit of despair.
They will be called oaks of righteousness,
    a planting of the Lord
    for the display of his splendor. . . .

'For I, the Lord, love justice;
   I hate robbery and iniquity.
In my faithfulness I will reward them
   and make an everlasting covenant with them' "
      (Isaiah 61:1-3, 8).

O Lord, may the Spirit that anointed Jesus also empower us to preach and be good news among the poor. May it bind us to bind the brokenhearted. May it free us to free the captives. May it release us from our own prisons so that we may release all those imprisoned in our world today, whether for acting justly or for acting in the desperation of poverty. May it comfort us when we grow discouraged in your cause, so that we may comfort other mourners. Together with your Spirit and with the poor, may we proclaim a new Jubilee, a new era of forgiven debts, land reform, freedom for all still enslaved, and a reprieve for the beleaguered earth itself.

This is our commission. This is the covenant we must make with you, the poor, and each other. We need your Spirit, Lord, to send and enable us. We need your grace to make a lasting covenant. We need your love so that we might love others. We need your faithfulness so that we may be faithful to the promises to you and to the poor that we have made as we have read, studied, prayed, and discussed.

And we need your Son Jesus Christ to show us love again, to teach us to die again, so that we may live again.

It is in his healing name we pray.

Amen.

● ● ●

Learning by Heart

If you are reading this book alone, write your own prayer in response to the *good news to the poor* that God has offered to you through this study.

If you are reading this book as part of a group study, plan a worship service in response to the *good news to the poor* that God has offered to you. The service may be for the group itself, and could include Eucharist, or communion, as a way of covenanting to continue working together to share Christ's life among the poor.

Or it can be for a special service in your congregation and be a way of sharing what God has been doing among you with others. In this case, you might ask the congregation to lay hands on your group and commission it to continue working for and among the poor.

Use the above texts from Isaiah, or other texts that have been particularly meaningful to you throughout this study. You may also want to follow the same outline: invocation, confession, proclamation, thanksgiving, and commissioning or covenant.

Making Connections

Written with
Jocele Meyer and Art Meyer,
Global Education Office,
Mennonite Central Committee U.S.,
and other MCC staff

Introduction

To Know Christ, Obey Him

AN OLD CHINESE proverb says: "Unless I act on what I know, I don't know even that." Or as the apostle John bluntly put it, "We know that we have come to know [Christ] if we obey his commands. The man who says, 'I know him,' but does not do what he commands is a liar, and the truth is not in him" (1 John 2:3-4).

If our knowledge of the Bible's teachings on relationship with people who are poor does not lead to obedience, we soon forget or quickly begin to deceive ourselves about our actions. Likewise, we must understand society to act rightly, but we must become socially active to really understand society at all. This does not mean our starting point is necessarily the frenzy that sometimes passes as activism. Jesus is our most important model, and he spent thirty years in anonymous labor, prayer, and reflection. Only then did he begin his short, yet world-transforming, public ministry.

However, Jesus' whole life was incarnation. In him, God identified with impoverished humanity through a direct personal relationship. That is why in sharing the Bible's call to turn toward people who are poor, I have emphasized changing the heart through a relationship with the poor—not simply changing your mind through information about poverty.

Information just does not come first.

Still, in living in a converted way and in bringing God's kingdom closer to the world around us, information and analysis are important. Part of incarnation is understanding each time and place into which God's good news enters. Without that to orient us, we may never get beyond good intentions. So now we need to give more attention to the causes of poverty in God's world today. This is the focus of part two: "Making Connections."

If you or your group followed the suggestions at the ends of chapters 3, 6, 7, and 10, you have begun to learn more about poverty in your area. You may even have started to make connections to global poverty. And you have found helpful the process outlined at the end of chapter 10 in the section "For Thought, Discussion, and Action." Now you want to learn more and begin to plan a response. There are various options:

1. *Perhaps you are considering a local response to poor people in your area,* but what you learned from part one is how much more you have to learn. To respond locally, you may sense a need to develop further relationships with poor people in your area; investigate the economy, housing, environment, and politics of the area; and find out who is already doing what with the poor. You may be struggling with the commitment of time, resources, and lifestyle-change that you sense a faithful response might entail. Therefore, you might want to retrace the tentative steps you have already taken. Go back to the suggestions at the ends of chapters 6, 7, 9, and 10. Week by week, repeat the suggestions in each one in greater depth.

2. *Perhaps you are realizing that your local area is connected to some global dimension of poverty in a particular way.* If unemployment, housing, or land use is a pressing local problem, you might want to take up to four sessions to work through chapter 12. If you are concerned that your local economy is too dependent on defense industries and arms production for export, take up to four sessions to work through chapter 13. If you sense God calling you to work for more faithful stewardship of nature, take up to four sessions to work through chap-

ter 14. If racial oppression or discrimination against women is a central concern as you look at local poverty, take up to four sessions to work through chapter 15.

To decide which of these areas of concern to respond to in depth, skim through chapters 12-15. They list seventeen different causes of poverty. Focus on the cluster of causes for poverty that matches your concerns most closely.

If you choose an in-depth response to one issue, you might give one week to each of the following:

● Answer the discussion questions based on the case study.

● Use the discussion questions based on the analysis section.

● Discuss how to network with other groups or national organizations working at the same concern.

● Plan your own response.

3. *Perhaps you are impressed with the interconnectedness of poverty around the globe.* You know that more study alone cannot take the place of a lived-out human response to people who are poor. But you want to work at the larger structural dimensions of poverty, and you need to prepare well. After all, you will face many diverse questions from other people as soon as you begin working for social change.

Give one week to each chapter in this section. You will probably not be able to cover all the material, but background reading is there for those who want it. In a group setting, you will probably want to dedicate session time to discussion questions that follow each case study or each analysis section. Later, when you decide on the dimension of poverty to which you feel most called to respond, you can return to the ideas and resources listed at the end of the appropriate chapter.

4. *Perhaps you have a special interest in the issues of poverty, injustice, human rights, and peace in a particular region of the world.* Even before you began this study, you may have encountered the stories and cases of particular people. You may know of organizations working at the issues in your region of concern. Chances are you are already actively involved in some way. Working through the analysis section in each chap-

ter may help you gain a new sense of which factors are most critical in that region and how they interconnect.

Whichever concern God is laying on your heart, I cannot emphasize enough the importance of working together with others in some kind of ongoing group. Among the action ideas listed in the remaining chapters are some that individuals or families can do. Even these will be more effective and enduring, however, if they spring from shared reflection and are sustained through mutual support and accountability. Besides, it is more fun if you have someone with whom to celebrate and weep, break bread and sing, pray and fast.

At the end of each chapter is a list of organizations that are working on the issues just discussed. You might contact these for networking, further learning, up-to-date information, and more action ideas. In addition, here are some organizations whose work cuts across various issues. The following groups are especially noteworthy because *they work nationally and have a network of state and local affiliates*:

• Bread for the World, 802 Rhode Island Avenue NE, Washington, D.C. 20018 (202-269-0200).

• National IMPACT, 100 Maryland Avenue NE, Washington, D.C. 20002 (202-544-8636).

To keep up with current legislation in the United States and Canada that may affect poverty and its causes, I suggest you contact the following organizations. The Friends Committee and the Washington Office of MCC both have regular newsletters:

• Friends Committee on National Legislation, 245 Second Street NE, Washington, D.C. 20002 (202-547-6000).

• Ottawa Office of Mennonite Central Committee Canada, 803-63 Sparks Street, Ottawa, Ont. K1P 5A6 (613-238-7224).

• Washington Office of Mennonite Central Committee U.S., 110 Maryland Avenue NE, #502, Washington, D.C. 20002 (202-544-6564).

Finally, if you would like *to organize fund-raising activities* for development projects that empower poor people overseas and in North America, you might contact one of the following organizations. Some also offer *service opportunities* for those who feel called to relocate and dedicate technical and professional skills to empowering the poor:

American Friends Service Committee, 1501 Cherry Street, Philadelphia, Pa. 19102-1479 (215-241-7000).

Canadian Friends Service Committee, 60 Lowther Avenue, Toronto, Ont. M5R 1C7 (416-920-5213).

Canadian Catholic Organization for Development and Peace, 3028 Danforth Avenue, Toronto, Ont. M4C 1N2 (416-651-9208).

Canadian Lutheran World Relief, 1829 Arlington Street, Winnipeg, Man. R2X 1W4 (204-586-8558).

Catholic Relief Services, 1011 First Avenue, New York, N.Y. 10022 (212-838-4700).

Church World Service, 475 Riverside Drive, New York, N.Y. 10115 (212-870-2257).

EIRENE, Engerser Street 74b, D5450 Neuweid-Rhein, West Germany.

Habitat for Humanity, Habitat and Church Streets, Americus, Ga. 31709-3498 (912-924-6935).

Heifer Project International, P.O. Box 808, 1015 South Louisiana, Little Rock, Ark. 72203 (501-376-6836).

Lutheran World Relief, 360 Park Avenue, New York, N.Y. 10010 (212-532-6350).

Mennonite Central Committee, 21 South 12th Street, P.O. Box 500, Akron, Pa. 17501-0500 (717-859-1151).

Mennonite Central Committee—Canada, 134 Plaza Drive, Winnipeg, Man. R3T 5K9 (204-261-6381).

OXFAM America, 115 Broadway, Boston, Mass. 02116 (617-482-1211).

OXFAM Canada, 251 Laurier Street W, Suite 301, Ottawa, Ont. K1P 5J6 (613-978-4725).

World Neighbors, 5116 North Portland Avenue, Oklahoma City, Okla. 73112 (405-946-3333).

12
Poverty and Economic Injustice

IN 1984, for the first time since 1978, Carlito Sumagpi worked his land. In 1978, Del Monte had plowed Carlito's field two feet deep and sprayed it with a potent herbicide. For years, Carlito said, not even the weeds grew on his land, let alone any crop he might have wanted to plant.

In 1974, Del Monte began an ambitious drive to expand its approximately 20,000-acre pineapple plantation in Bukidnon province in the Philippines. Some small farmers were happy to sign long-term leases, turning their land over to the company in exchange for an annual fee. Others claim that the company's armed security guards threatened and intimidated them. Some farmers say Del Monte cattle were deliberately chased onto their fields. Several people had roads bulldozed across their land. And since hardly any of the farmers could read the complex English-language contract they were asked to sign, there are accusations that Del Monte agents, eager to earn commissions, lied about its contents.

As an incentive, Del Monte promised to employ on its plantation any farmer willing to lease her or his land. Now many farmers complain of being laid off. The company says that these people could not handle the discipline that the work required.

Carlito's case is somewhat different. The land in the Del Monte expansion area belongs largely to members of the Higaonon tribe, who have lived there for decades. Many of these farmers had never bothered to apply for land titles. They saw little reason to spend time and money obtaining a piece of paper they could not read to prove they owned land on which their families had always lived. Carlito tried to acquire a title; but after several trips to the provincial capital, he realized he did not have the cash or the political connections necessary for the process.

When Del Monte's expansion plans became known, land speculators with government connections and money to pay bribes were able to acquire land titles. Carlito found his land literally leased out from under him. Fortunately, with the assistance of his community and local church workers, Carlito was able to take his case to court. The judge ruled in Carlito's favor, and Del Monte had to return his land to him. But the damage had been done. For six years, Carlito says, his six acres of land yielded no crops. Del Monte paid him fifty dollars as compensation.

Carlito Sumagpi is one of the fortunate ones. Community and church support gave him courage to claim his rights. The court system actually worked for him. He still has land. More often foreign corporations and powerful Filipino plantation owners have bent the law to their purposes. According to OXFAM America, when Ferdinand Marcos ruled the Philippines, his government once placed an ad in a U.S. business journal: "To attract companies like yours . . . we have felled mountains, razed jungles, filled swamps, moved rivers, relocated towns, and in their place built power plants, dams, roads. . . . All to make it easier for you and your business to do business here."[1]

Unfortunately, the boast was no exaggeration. What the ad conveniently omitted was that people were part of the dislocation. Deception, threats, and violence have moved them off the land to make way for export crops to fund development and hydroelectric dams to power it. But development of what? The Philippines is the world's number-one producer of pineapples and number-three producer of bananas. Yet a 1982 government survey estimated that 70 percent of the school-children were undernourished.[2]

Although a nonviolent movement for reform and democracy forced Marcos from power in 1986, too little has changed. Since the 1950s, each new government has promised land reform but has failed to deliver. A majority of the Philippines' 61 million people live in rural areas. Some seventy-five percent of rural families earn less than $125 per family per month, the official poverty line. In some areas, the situation is worse. In the early 1980s, the magic of cash crops for export disappeared. For example, sugar turned sour as world prices plummeted. On the lush island of Negros, many sugar plantation owners stopped producing, leaving over half the workers without employment.

● ● ●

For Discussion

1. Divide a chalkboard or newsprint into four sections. Write one of these words at the top of each box: Economic, Religious, Political, Other. Think of things that link you to Carlito, and list each under one of the four categories.

2. What rights do you enjoy that Carlito could *not* count on? In what ways are you, or people you know personally, also vulnerable like Carlito and other Filipino peasants? On what, then, does economic security depend?

3. Do you know any North American farmers who have lost their land recently? Do you know any North American workers who have lost their jobs recently? To what degree was economic injustice a factor? How might a more just economy in North America have prevented those situations?

Global Economic Causes of Poverty

We have often heard it before: The rich get richer, and the poor get poorer. But others object. Though the rich get rich faster, they insist, overall economic growth means the poor also are doing better. As John F. Kennedy once explained the theory, a rising tide lifts all boats, large and small.

In the 1960s, the world economic tide may have been rising. But since then, the smaller boats have contended with gale-force winds and proven leaky, while larger boats have docked in relative safety. Optimistic economic plans for developing countries have gone sour, debt has locked them into decline, and the gap between rich and poor has grown.

Twenty-five years ago the average citizen of the noncommunist *North* was twenty times better off than the average citizen in low-income regions like India, Bangladesh, and much of Africa. By the late 1970s, the figure was forty times. By the mid-1980s, according to World Bank data, it was forty-six times! The United States Census Bureau reported in 1989 that the wealthiest 20 percent of the people received 44 percent of the income. The gap between upper- and lower-income families is now wider than at any time since the bureau began collecting these data in 1947.

But were the poor getting poorer? From 1980 to 1985 gross domestic product (GDP) per capita rose in the developed countries by 8 percent, despite a recession in 1981-82. In underdeveloped countries of the *South,* per capita GDP *fell* by 7.5 percent. In Africa it fell by 11 percent; in the Middle East by 19.2 percent.

So the gap has widened in both directions. People in the third world make up 75 percent of the world's population but receive only 17 percent of world GNP (gross national product). The wealthy 20 percent of the rich nations receive nearly 70 percent of the world's income. We are seeing dramatic increases in the rich-poor gap both *within* countries like the United States and Canada and *between* nations of the first and third worlds.

A critical question, however, is whether the rich getting richer *cause* the poor to get poorer. Economists have long debated the question, and this book is not going to resolve it. You will have to reach your own conclusions.

But remember what we said in the first part of this book: Poverty has as much to do with power and exclusion as with money. The poor are the powerless ones at the margins of society. What statistics and economic flow charts can only dimly reflect is that those with more money also have more power to exercise their will over those who are weaker. Hence, injustice.

Where there is plenty of food, people still go hungry because they do not have money to buy it. Where the environment is misused and where there are natural catastrophes, only the poor go hungry or homeless. Hence, exploitation and related causes of poverty.

Cause 1: Lack of Employment

First, let's not overlook the obvious: people need work to buy bread. In many third world countries, unemployment exceeds 50 percent of the potential work force. In the U.S., the figure for many minority youth is about the same. Poverty is inevitable where such unemployment levels exist.

If rural people are to work, they always need land and often need credit or extension services. If urban people are to work, they need either jobs or capital for their own small businesses and cottage industries. If people are in transition between rural and urban life, or if the urban economy itself is in transition, they usually need education and training for employment.

But again, what is at stake is power. Unemployment does not just happen. It causes poverty, but it also is *caused.* All the remaining causes (described below) contribute.

Cause 2: Exploitation of the Poor by the Wealthy and Powerful

What happened to Filipino peasants like Carlito happens to other people. Those with power and resources write the laws or find ways around the laws. They set prices for goods and loans. Peasants from Bangladesh to Guatemala often have no choice but to turn to local loan sharks who charge usurious interest rates of well over 100 percent a year.

In the Philippines, a powerful company *moved in* and took over control of the land. Sometimes the powerful can flex their muscles by *moving out,* or merely threatening to do so. Plants that have provided work for generations of workers in a community may suddenly shut down and move on. The companies that own them negotiate with towns, states or provinces, and foreign countries for tax breaks and other advantages. Lately, the practice of pitting one region against another in the name of competitiveness has received increasing attention in North America. But companies working overseas have often overwhelmed local governments with threats to move elsewhere in search of cheaper labor.

Cause 3: Unfair World Trade and Monetary Systems

After World War II, the U.S. was in a position to control world trade, setting prices for raw materials and regulations for finished materials. Before that, colonial powers had control. Now Europe and Japan challenge U.S. ascendancy, but together these countries still have enormous advantages over third-world countries. Furthermore, multinational corporations with great influence on industrial governments continue to call the shots on many trade and banking regulations.[3]

The poor have little chance. In 1954, a sugar-producing country like the Dominican Republic could buy one tractor with 24 tons of sugar. By 1982, it took 115 tons of sugar. Countries producing products like sugar, bananas, and coffee have failed in their attempts to form cartels that might negotiate prices with richer countries rather than bidding each other down.

One result of collapsing prices for commodities that poorer countries have to sell has been mounting debt throughout the third world. In the 1960s and 70s, banks in the richer nations encouraged many countries to borrow heavily for development projects—and arms. But then their anticipated export earnings shrunk. Earnings that were to have been reinvested in new industries are not only smaller, but must go to repay debts. Interest payments in Latin America consume more than one third of export earnings.

Meanwhile, if countries are to remain solvent, they must often negotiate new debts. The International Monetary Fund (IMF) in effect determines their credit ratings and has the power to demand domestic austerity measures to insure repayment. Governments must cut back investment in their most valuable resource—people—through cuts in education, health care, and other social services. For example, in 1984 the IMF demanded that Brazil export at least 700,000 tons of beef if it wanted further access to international financing. That same year, a thousand children under five died daily in Brazil due to diseases resulting from malnutrition.

Brazil is just one example. In late 1988, the United Nations Children's Fund (UNICEF) estimated that 500,000 children had died in the previous twelve months as a *direct* result of third-world countries transferring their money to richer nations to service their debts. Many more died indirectly from the world's misplaced priorities. In that same year, 13 million children under age five died, many of preventable illnesses.

Cause 4: Modern Western Agriculture and Agribusiness

All around the world, land is being concentrated in the hands of fewer and fewer people. The process began with European colonization of Africa, Latin America, and Asia. In Latin America especially, Spain and Portugal developed large feudalistic plantations owned by a few. But today multinational agribusinesses, in collaboration with local governments, have taken over. Even in the U.S. and Canada, corporations are consolidating more and more farmland. Without access to land—a place to live and to grow food—people become more vulnerable to the whims of the rich and powerful.

Thirty-six of the world's poorest countries export food to North America, according to OXFAM America. In the Caribbean, 50 percent of the population is undernourished, while 50 percent of the land grows export crops like coffee, sugar, and bananas.

In many poor countries, multinational companies and local elites have purchased the better land—often at low prices—to grow such cash crops as peanuts, coffee, bananas, tea, pineapples, sugar, and flowers for export to already-rich countries. The poor must raise their crops on marginal land or depend on cash cropping and seasonal farm work for jobs. But these jobs become fewer as mechanization by the companies increases. This process also hurts U.S. workers who lose jobs to operations in other countries.

Cause 5: Overconsumption of Natural Resources by the Rich

Unjust economics makes overconsumption by rich nations possible, but overconsumption also contributes to further inequities. North Americans constitute about 5 percent of the world's people. They use 35 percent of the world's oil, 33 percent of its minerals and energy, 44 percent of its coal, and 61 percent of its natural gas. If all the world's farmers farmed like North Americans do, the world would be out of oil in eleven years.[4] Overconsumption and extravagant living keeps the poor in the third world poor.

• • •

For Further Discussion

4. What words and images do you associate with the idea of development? On chalkboard or newsprint, make two lists. On one side list positive associations; on the other side, negative associations. Then discuss: What must be present for development to improve the lives of the poor? What would Carlito say?

5. In 1986, a World Bank study on *Poverty and Hunger* stated: "The world has ample food. The growth of global food production has been faster than the unprecedented population growth of the past forty years. . . . Yet many poor countries and hundreds of millions of poor people do not share in this abundance. They suffer from a lack of food security, caused

mainly by a lack of purchasing power."[5]

If the cause of hunger and poverty is *not* shortage, but poor distribution and lack of purchasing power, what are the implications for relief and development organizations trying to end poverty and hunger? What priorities and strategies would you recommend to them?

6. Are the poor getting poorer *because* the rich are getting richer?

● ● ●

Scriptures for Reflection

As you read, study, and discuss the following texts, consider the perspective you believe a Filipino peasant like Carlito would have: Isaiah 3:13-20; Amos 8:4-6; Micah 2:1-2; and James 5:1-6.

● ● ●

Ideas for Action

1. Choose volunteers to research nearby cases of farm foreclosure or factories moving elsewhere, talk to those affected, and report back. Explore ways to support those affected. Investigate current legislation dealing with such issues. Write to editors and government representatives.

2. Sponsor a community-wide awareness day concerning homelessness and poverty. Invite local organizations that empower the poor and homeless to set up displays and to speak on programs for housing, employment, and other services for people in need. Also ask local legislators to report on their initiatives. Contact the national office of your denomination or faith community to learn about resources and programs on issues of homelessness, poverty, and employment.

3. On a regular basis work in a small soup kitchen or shelter where it is possible to develop friendships with the poor. Find out where poor people in your community go for health care. In the U.S. the experience of going to a poor people's health clinic graphically shows the country's two-tier health-

care system. Join a coalition of the homeless or other poor peoples' groups where you sit as equals, rather than in a charity relationship.

4. Join a study-and-action tour in North America or to a third-world country. Tours that emphasize action during and following the experience are preferred. Some organizations offering such tours are listed at the end of the introduction to part two: "To Know Christ, Obey Him." So do the Center for Global Education, Augsburg College, 731 Twenty-First Avenue South, Minneapolis, Minn. 55454 (612-330-1159); and Synapses, listed below.

5. Examine your buying habits for a month by listing all purchases. Where are the items produced? Does their production take unfair advantage of workers and farmers or subject them to poor working conditions? A helpful resource for answering such questions is *Rating America's Corporate Conscience: A Provocative Guide to the Companies Behind the Products You Buy Every Day,* by Steven Lydenberg of the Council on Economic Priorities, 30 Irving Place, New York, N.Y. 10003 (212-420-1133).

After a month, consider changes. Reduce wasteful consumption, and favor companies that treat workers fairly. Impose a 10 percent *tax* on yourself when you purchase luxury items or imports from the third world, such as bananas or coffee. Then give this money to an overseas development agency. A helpful resource for making changes is *Add Justice to Your Shopping List: A Guide for Reshaping Food Buying Habits,* a 70-page booklet written by Marilyn Helmuth Voran for the Mennonite Central Committee U.S., Office on Global Education, 21 South 12th Street, Akron, Pa. 17501 (717-859-1151), and published in 1986 by Herald Press, Scottdale, Pa. 15683.

6. Increase the effectiveness of changing your personal economic system by participating in boycotts of products and companies that represent particularly oppressive or destructive practices. Declaring your church a zone free of the product being boycotted will increase the educational value of the effort. For information on current boycotts, write to the *National Boycott Newsletter,* 6505 Twenty-eighth Avenue NE, Seattle, Wash. 98115.

• • •

To Keep Connecting

Debt Crisis Network, c/o Institute for Policy Studies, 1601
Connecticut Avenue NW, Washington, D.C. 20009 (202-
234-9382). Coalition of church, hunger, development,
research, and farm organizations concerned about the
impact of the international debt crisis on people, particularly in the third world.

Interfaith Action for Economic Justice, 110 Maryland Avenue
NE, Suite 509, Washington, D.C. 20002-5694 (202-543-
2800). Advocate for greater justice for the needy.
Provides background on legislative issues.

Interfaith Center for Corporate Responsibility, 475 Riverside
Drive, Room 566, New York, N.Y. 10115 (212-870-2295).
Provides a variety of publications such as *The Corporate
Examiner* and services for alternative investments.

Synapses, 1821 W. Cullerton, Chicago, Ill. 60608 (312-421-
5513). Interfaith grassroots organization working for
justice, peace, and spirituality. Members contribute one
half day a month for activities on behalf of people in the
Philippines, Southeast Asia, Southern Africa, and Central
America.

Taskforce on the Churches and Corporate Responsibility, 129
St. Clair Avenue West, Toronto, Ont. M4V 1N5 (416-
923-1758). Coalition of Canadian churches addressing
issues of corporate responsibility and Canadian foreign
policy in the area of human rights and social justice.

Ten Days for World Development, 85 St. Clair Avenue East,
Room 315, Toronto, Ont. M4T 1M8 (416-922-0591).
Interchurch program for development education and
action sponsored by the relief and development agencies
of the Anglican, Catholic, Lutheran, Presbyterian, and
United Churches in Canada. Highlights a specific area of
need for study and action each year.

Notes

1. OXFAM America, *The Philippines: A Harvest of Anger* (Boston: OXFAM America, 1987), p. 5.

2. For information, see Frances M. Lappé and Joseph Collins, *Food First* (Westminster, Md.: Ballantine, 1981); and Joseph Collins, *Philippines: Fire on the Rim* (San Francisco: Institute for Food and Development Policy, 1989).

3. Cf. Ronald J. Sider, *Rich Christians in an Age of Hunger: A Biblical Study* (Downers Grove, Ill.: InterVarsity Press, 1977), pp. 131-67; and Frances Moore Lappé and Joseph Collins, *Food First: Beyond the Myth of Scarcity* (Boston: Houghton Mifflin Co., 1977), pp. 181-209.

4. C. Dean Freudenberger, *Food for Tommorrow?* (Minneapolis: Augsburg, 1984), p. 64, referring to David Pimentel and Marcia Pimentel, *Food, Energy and Society* (New York: Halsted Press, 1979), p. 137.

5. *Poverty and Hunger: Issues and Options for Food Security in Developing Countries* (A World Bank Policy Study, 1986), p. 1.

13

Poverty, Militarism, and War

"A FEW YEARS back we arrived in Moriah [in southeastern Honduras] as a small group of families working there and seeking unity. We met the Lord there. We were growing as a Christian community and also working together in material things. Our principal objective was to improve the land, develop some good coffee farms, raise cattle. There were years of prosperity without so much as a rumor of war—no *contras* [Nicaragua counterrevolutionaries], or anything of the sort.

"We were doing well in material goods. We had furniture, a few wire fences, pigs, chickens; and some of the families had cows. Maybe they only had a few, but they had enough to start herds. Together we had improved the roads so that we could bring in food supplies by mule. The truth is, it was a good setting. After I started pastoring in the city of Danlí, my brothers came to help me manage the work. I even had a small business there in Moriah selling provisions for people who worked in nearby mines. We sold sugar, soap—basic things people need. This gave the family a little extra income.

"Then all this fell apart. In March of 1986, there was heavy combat right near Moriah, though not in the community of Moriah itself. There are two mountain ridges not far away where the contras had built a well-fortified camp. It was a training base.

"During Holy Week, the Sandinista army advanced from Nicaragua and attacked the contras. They had what people call rocket launchers. When those rockets echo in the mountains, they sound very loud, like bombs; and when they go off, they strike terror in your heart. No one died in Moriah. But out of fear, people began to flee. They thought to themselves: 'Well, right now the fighting is right over there; tomorrow mortars will be landing here.' They only took a few basics—a few clothes to cover themselves. Some took a couple of mules and left everything else.

"Retreating contras showed up in Moriah, as did civilians fleeing fierce battles closer to the border. They looted and ate everything up in our little stores. We lost everything that my brother left behind in the house—rice, potatoes, corn. Some houses were left completely bare. Everyone who came through was looking for refuge. They took over the pastures, and their animals ate up all the grass. They ruined the wire fences. The area practically turned into a desert again. Everything started growing over, since no one was there to take care of the fields. The roads are impassable. Only armed people frequent them. The few souls who remain aren't working except to subsist. No one is improving the roads or their properties because they are afraid of more battles. So in this way, poverty is taking over.

"When families fled, some sold out at dirt prices. People with a few more resources bought their properties for a quarter of what they were worth. This meant the financial ruin of many brothers and sisters in the church. They took refuge in better protected towns close by. But the little bit of money from what they had sold didn't last long at all because things are more expensive in town. They didn't have enough money, and they were left without work.

"Myself? Now I've lost the income from my little business. I've had trouble coming up with the funds to enroll my girls in school. I still have my little coffee farm. The coffee beans ripened this year as usual, but the quality was down. And I didn't have anyone to help me harvest it, since people are afraid and don't want to go back and work. The property just gives us headaches. We'd like to sell, but it has deteriorated and is worth even less. Our work there is now a total bust.

"What have we learned? Well, we sometimes think that all this suffering is part of the fulfillment of the Scriptures, which say that times of war and rumors of war will come. But we always believed that this would happen in some other place! We never thought here. We could look on all this as an act of God's will, a punishment for someone or other. But in fact, these are things that we can never really understand. I guess our hopes have gotten whittled down."

• • •

For Discussion

1. Obviously the most dramatic effect of warfare is violent death. But even though no one in the village of Moriah died, war undermined the life-support system of Moriah in many ways. List all the ways that you can discover in the case study.

2. When the Honduran pastor told his story, he was struggling with how to understand the suffering his family, church, and community had experienced. He admits that when such suffering happened only to other people far away, it was easier to say, "It's God's will," or call it the fulfillment of scriptural prophecies. Now he confronts the age-old question, "Why do the righteous suffer?" And he is not so sure. Do you have any counsel for him?

3. Are you as far away from the suffering of war as this pastor once thought he was? How might North Americans be connected to this suffering even though it seems far away? What counsel do you think this pastor would have for you?

War and Militarism as Causes of Poverty

"Each year the world spends several times as much on research to increase the destructiveness of weapons as on attempts to raise the productivity of agriculture. Indeed, expenditures on weapons research, in which a half-million scientists are now employed, exceed the combined spending on developing new energy technologies, improving human health, raising agricultural productivity, and controlling pollution."[1]

Increasing militarization of society is having a disastrous affect on the quality of human life around the world. Since 1945, 120 wars—and preparation for more—have diverted essential resources from programs for human development. As a result, poverty, hunger, and oppression have escalated. The connections between militarization and development, at home and abroad, are manifold.

It is difficult to comprehend the dramatic increases in worldwide military spending in the recent decade. In 1987, the world spent over $1 trillion on armaments and defense— almost twenty times pre-World War II budgets. This is more money than the poorest half of the world's people earn in one year.

The United States and the Soviet Union still lead the arms race. Together they comprise just 11 percent of the world's population but account for over 50 percent of the world's military expenditures. The two superpowers each spend nearly $300 billion annually for defense. This represents 6.4 percent of the U.S. gross national product (GNP) and 14 percent of the Soviet GNP.

The industrialized countries of the world are the biggest military spenders. They include less than 25 percent of the world's people but spend more than 75 percent of the world's arms budget. But the most rapid growth in recent military spending has been in some parts of the third world. Along with this growth has come military rule. Ruth Leger Sivard reported that between 1960 and 1985 the number of nations ruled by military governments grew from 22 to 57.[2]

Most of the world's hungry, poor, and refugees are in the third world. Since 1945, that is where the world's wars, revolutions, and conflicts have been. For example, the five countries in Africa that suffered the most desperate hunger in the 1980s were engaged in conflict: Ethiopia, Mozambique, Angola, Somalia, Sudan. This is no accident. War causes hunger and poverty. In turn, poor, hungry people kindle revolution.

Militarism permeates world society today. It has disastrous effects on all of humanity's most important problems—hunger, poverty, oppression, and environmental degradation. Militarization of society tangles up practically every relief, development, and justice issue both at home and abroad. It does its damage by:

- Diverting resources from human needs.
- Tempting governments to solve domestic problems through military solutions.
- Disrupting life-support systems wherever open warfare breaks out.

Cause 6: Preparation for War

Placed next to development efforts, world military expenditures reveal misdirected priorities. Sivard points out that in 1984, world military expenditures for each soldier averaged $28,494. During that same year, the United States spent $105,638 per soldier and $792 per student. Canada spent (U.S.) $94,878 per soldier and $983 per schoolchild.

Between 1970 and 1980, the total value of arms imported by developing countries grew 400 percent, from $3.9 billion to $19.5 billion. Population in these countries, by comparison, grew 25 percent. For the hungry people in these nations, this military buildup means diminished hope for a better life. Money spent on arms is money that cannot be spent on the needs of people. Military aid creates debt and dependency. Military forces are often used to repress poor people—and others working on their behalf.

Some claim that military spending is good for the economy. It is, but for few people. Data from the U.S. Bureau of Labor Statistics reveal that $1 billion invested in defense industry creates only 75,000 jobs. The same amount invested in civil engineering creates 110,000 jobs; in health care systems, 138,000 jobs; and in education 138,000 jobs.

In the third world, the trade-off between guns and butter is often even more direct. Of the third world's $950 billion debt burden, 25 percent is for arms. Theoretically, when countries borrow money for economic development projects, they should be able to earn back enough to pay off their debt and more. But when countries run up their international debts importing arms, they only go into the hole. None of the loan money gets invested in productive activities or even recycled in the local economy.

Cause 7: Repression and Internal Warfare

"The third world war has already begun—in the third world," a senior government minister from Singapore said in 1985. "The new war is likely to be a culmination of little wars rather than one big war between the great powers and one fought for the realization of their ambitions and the promotion of their national interests. However, this is not obvious because in this new world war, the great powers are invisible."

While some of these "little wars" involve one third-world country against another—the Iran-Iraq War is a particularly brutal example—most of these wars are internal. In the 1980s, ethnic warfare pitted the government of Ethiopia against the Eritreans, the government of Sri Lanka against the Sikhs, the government of Indonesia against the people of East Timor, and so on. Religion complicated some of these conflicts, as it did in Lebanon and Northern Ireland. Guerrilla warfare provoked government reaction in countries like those of Central America, Southern Africa, Afghanistan, the Philippines, Peru.

Such wars do not respond chiefly to external threats. Foreign powers do sometimes seek to manipulate events to their advantage. Yet in order to justify repression of their own people and win military aid from superpower allies, dictators and military governments often label all internal challenges to their power as externally inspired.

In Latin America, a "Doctrine of National Security" turns the poor into potential enemies of the state. It defines even nonviolent protest as subversive, and therefore part of an "international communist conspiracy." In Argentina in the 1970s, the military regime in power captured, tortured, and killed 15,000 to 30,000 people in the name of stamping out communist subversion. But no more than 200 were guerrillas. A military pamphlet even included the Lion's Club in what it called the "tree of subversion."

Repressive military action can never solve economic and social problems that result when the poor are deprived of land, exploited economically, or mistreated because of their race. Even conflicts such as the one in Lebanon, known as a religious war, arise largely from economic disparities.

Abundant arms tempt even civilian governments to try to squelch efforts for change without addressing problems that make the status quo intolerable. Military dictatorships are likely to confuse the causes and symptoms of social conflict entirely. In 1987, militaries controlled over half of third-world governments. All but two of these fifty-nine governments were systematically violating citizens' rights.

Cause 8: Open Warfare

The rich desire military security to protect their own wealth and status. But the fighting that results is a major cause of poverty. War and revolution have displaced millions of people. As in Honduras, those who flee from conflictive areas often leave with only what they can carry.

Where people need emergency food aid, war hinders food distribution. It also hinders development work. War destroys the environment. In a talk at Cornell University in 1982, Roger Shinn, professor of social ethics at Union Theological Seminary in New York, stated: "War, along with everything else that is said about it, remains the most ecologically destructive of all human activities."

War displaces and concentrates populations and reduces or eliminates traditional trade patterns. War increases health problems. As public services break down, refugees must seek makeshift shelters; and refugee camps become easy targets for epidemics. War disrupts family and community life.

• • •

For Further Discussion

4. During the 1980s, the United States and the Soviet Union each spent roughly $2 trillion on defense. That equals $1 billion for each in every year since the birth of Christ. It adds up to over $9,000 for each U.S. and Soviet citizen. How much is $2 trillion? These comparisons offer a mental picture:

- $1 million—a stack of $1,000-bills four inches high.
- $1 billion—a stack of $1,000-bills 333 feet high.
- $2 trillion—a stack of $1,000-bills 134 miles high.

5. Ruth Leger Sivard writes, "It is difficult to find among today's most pressing issues any that lend themselves to military solutions. In this sense military power seems to be irrelevant to national and global security."[3] Do you agree that military expenditures contribute little or nothing to humanity's most pressing problems? That military power will not provide true security? On what does human security depend?

6. Are there military bases or military-related industries in your town or region of the country? Do they make you feel more secure or less secure? How would you go about determining whether these facilities contribute more or less to your local economy than a comparable investment in civilian industries, education, or public services like health care?

• • •

Scriptures for Reflection

As you read and discuss the following texts, paraphrase them for modern situations you know about. For example, the first text refers to Egypt and chariots. Today, "Egypt" might be a superpower or some other ally, and "chariots" a powerful modern weapon. Also, remember to include the perspective of a war refugee such as those described (above) by the Honduran pastor as you study Isaiah 31:1, 3; James 4:1-3; and 2 Samuel 2:18-28.

• • •

Ideas for Action

1. Create a working group on economic conversion within the congregation or community. There are approximately 35,000 private companies that have prime military contracts with the U.S. Department of Defense. Even small communities in the U.S. and Canada host companies that produce weapons components. Workers involved in military-related production often face psychological pressures and difficult ethical dilemmas as part of their daily work experience.

Find out how military spending affects the local economy. What are the needs in the local area—for example, housing, education, employment? How might military dollars be spent for life rather than death? After the working group does some homework and generates initial proposals for shifting the local economy toward productive industries, hold a conference on economic conversion. Invite local clergy, business people, labor leaders, and the public to a day of lectures and workshops on economic conversion. Publicize your findings through letters to the editor of local papers, a bill in city council, and vigils if necessary.

If you would like a model for such an effort, write for a fifty-page report called *World Peace Begins in Lancaster,* available through MCC Peace Section, 21 South 12th Street, Akron, Pa. 17501 (717-859-1151). This report tells of Lancaster County Peacework Alternatives, a project that has sought to inform county residents of the economic and ethical problems of militarism at a local level.

One shortcut for any U.S. nonprofit organization that can raise $150 is to order a computerized listing of all the companies in your county with prime military contracts, the dollar value of those contracts, and what they are producing. County-by-county listings are available from Military Spending Research Services, P.O. Box 1794, 10 W. Washington Street, Middleburg, Va. 22117 (703-687-6777).

2. In election years, organize a candidates' forum. Ask candidates to speak to issues of economic conversion and

military planning. Voice the concern of the community over lopsided priorities and spending.

3. Learn alternative ways of defending human life while resisting current militaristic forms of defense. Form a local Christian Peacemaker Team (see below).

4. Communicate with officials often. Call, write, or visit. Legislative offices generally consider each letter to be the voice of 500 constituents. You might even form a prayer-and-letter-writing unit in your church to meet monthly, discuss the news, and write to legislators on behalf of a certain country, a specific policy, a particular issue, like nuclear disarmament. You may request a hearing from your congress-person or Member of Parliament in a district or riding office nearby.

5. The treatment of individual dissidents, religious leaders, and social-change activists in a given country usually reflects its government's respect for human rights in general. Holding governments accountable for their treatment of such individuals is one way to put a brake on repression and military control. Well-known human rights networks:

• Amnesty International, P.O. Box 1270, Nederland, Colo. 80466; and 294 Albert Street, Suite 204, Ottawa, Ont. K1P 6E6.

• The Christian Urgent Action Network, 1821 West Cullerton Street, Chicago, Ill. 60608, is currently focusing on El Salvador and the Philippines. It operates a telegram and telephone network on behalf of victims of human rights abuses there.

6. Sponsor an after-school program teaching peace-and-justice curriculum and offering noncompetitive ways of play. Plan an evening or weekend seminar for parents of participating children. Contact: Parenting for Peace and Justice, NNPJN, 4144 Lindell Boulevard, St. Louis, Mo. 63108.

7. Write for a list of large corporations with military contracts. Three sources:

• *The Corporate Examiner,* Interfaith Center for Corporate Responsibility, 475 Riverside Drive, Room 566, New York, N.Y. 10115 (212-870-2295).

● The Council on Economic Priorities, 30 Irving Place, New York, N.Y. 10003 (212-420-1133).

● The Task Force on The Churches and Corporate Responsibility, 129 St. Clair Avenue West, Toronto, Ont. M4V 2N5 (416-923-1758).

Note brand-name merchandise manufactured by such corporations. Can you purchase products from companies that have fewer military contracts, or none?

8. Familiarize yourself with your nation's annual budget, especially comparing amounts spent for the military with that spent for helping programs. Some people may want to speak against the amount of personal income taxes that fund military expenditures by limiting the amount of income tax they pay. This can be done by earning below the taxable level or making large tax-deductible donations. Others pay the military portion under protest or refuse to pay that portion, giving it instead to a charitable cause. A regularly updated information packet, *Christian Perspectives on War Tax Opposition,* is available from MCC U.S. Peace Section, 21 South 12th Street, Akron, Pa. 17501 (717-859-1151).

● ● ●

To Keep Connecting

Center for Economic Conversion, 222 View Street, Suite C, Mountain View, Calif. 94041 (415-968-8798). Functions as a resource to local groups. Resources include *The Military in Your Backyard: How to Determine the Impact of Military Spending in Your Community.*

Christian Peacemaker Teams, 1821 West Cullerton Street, Chicago, Ill. 60608 (312-421-5513). Ministry of Christian peace action among Mennonite and Brethren churches, applying the art of nonviolent direction action, in addition to research, prayer, negotiation, and careful organizing efforts, to creatively witness and work for peace from local to international levels.

Jobs with Peace Campaign, 76 Summer Street, Boston, Mass. 02110 (617-338-5783). Works on legislation favoring

economic conversion for jobs in healthy market
economies. Active state chapters throughout the U.S.
Project Ploughshares, Conrad Grebel College, Waterloo, Ont.
N2L 3G6 (519-888-6541). Investigates the economic and
political consequences of militarism, with a focus on
Canada.

Notes

1. Lester R. Brown and others, *State of the World 1986: A Worldwatch Institute Report on Progress Toward a Sustainable Society* (New York: W. W. Norton & Company, 1986), p. 199.

2. Ruth Leger Sivard, *World Military and Social Expenditures, 1985* (Washington, D.C.: World Priorities, 1985), p. 25.

3. Ruth Leger Sivard, *World Military and Social Expenditures, 1987-88* (Washington, D.C.: World Priorities, 1988), p. 21.

14
Poverty and Environmental Degradation

MR. ADOU, a farmer in central Nigeria, remembers that hunger was never far away when he was a boy. In his lifetime, he has seen prosperity come to his family and progress come to Nigeria. Fertilizers have improved crop yields. An oil boom has meant more vehicles, new roads, and greater markets for grain and produce. Now starvation is a rarity in his region.

But there are signs that this prosperity is beginning to erode—a victim of its own success. A growing population has taxed natural resources. The oil boom allowed Nigeria to import wheat, which kept local prices down for farmers. Both consumers and producers began to depend on imported materials that were cheap in the 1970s but sharply more expensive in the 1980s.

To feed a growing population and to keep up with a changing economy, farming has become more intense. This is straining the environment. It now takes more money to buy fertilizer and other inputs, so farms must be bigger. Farmers used to rotate their crops. Now they tend to grow the same crop year after year. Locusts are less of a problem, thanks to insecticides. But in some parts of Nigeria, clean drinking water is limited. Trees have fallen victim to increased demand for both land and firewood.

The result of all this is soil erosion, changing weather patterns, and a nagging question: Grateful as one is for life-improving changes, can they last? Let's listen:

Question: How long have you lived in this area?

Mr. Adou: I was born here, but left for another town and then returned here again. I am fifty-five. There are many changes.

Q: How big is your family?

Mr. Adou: In my own family, I have about eleven children.

Q: There must be a lot more people living here now than when you were a boy of twelve years.

Mr. Adou: Yes, it is much more full. There are changes in almost everything.

Q: How big is your farm? What crops are you growing?

Mr. Adou: It is a very large farm. We grow beans, sweet potatoes, sugarcane, tomatoes, onions, cabbage, and other local foods. I am also growing some fruit trees—orange, banana, wawa, mango.

Q: So you have a very wide variety of crops. You are able to sell some of the crops?

Mr. Adou: Yes, I send them out.

Q: So you have enough to feed your own family plus extra to sell. When you were a boy, did they grow all the crops that you are growing now?

Mr. Adou: In those days, in some parts of the year, we lived on leaves, something like spinach. There was a lot of hunger in those days. Now there is a lot of everything. Now with the introduction of fertilizer, people can grow a lot more food.

Q: I am interested to know if there has been any change in the climate also during the time that you've lived here.

Mr. Adou: There used to be heavy rainfall in those days. It has diminished a lot. In those days it would start raining around the end of March and continue through November.

Q: That's quite a contrast. I think this year the rains didn't start until early June and ended about the middle of October. Have there also been any changes in the vegetation that you've seen in the last fifty years or so? Are there fewer trees? Is there a change in the types of grasses that are here?

Mr. Adou: There is a great change in the vegetation. There used to be a lot of trees. Then people started to cut down the trees to plow for farming. There used to be less grass, because they didn't use fertilizer in those days. So now that there's a lot of fertilizer, the farm grows a lot of grass.

Q: Is the grass beneficial at all, or is it just a problem that you have to get rid of it?

Mr. Adou: Yes, it's really a problem. A person's garden and things can get swallowed by grass.

Q: It means that you've got a lot of weeding.

Mr. Adou: Yes, we have to weed it often.

Q: What about getting trees for firewood? Is that getting to be a problem too?

Mr. Adou: It is hard to get firewood because so many trees have been cut down. You can get it, but you have to go into the bush.

Q: I'm wondering if there are any changes in the cultural practices in terms of farming? You've mentioned that you're using a lot more fertilizer now than you used to and that has increased your yields substantially. For a farmer who can't afford fertilizer, his yields won't do so well.

Mr. Adou: Yes, not all of them can afford to buy the fertilizer.

Q: So they are going to remain pretty poor if they can't afford to buy fertilizer?

Mr. Adou: Yes, they pretty much get enough to eat, but no extra to sell.

Q: Has there been any change in the livestock populations since you were a boy? Are there more or less sheep, cattle, or goats? And what about the wildlife, the wild animals?

Mr. Adou: In those days there used to be a lot of animals in the bush, but there are so many hunters. There is not so much wildlife around. There are a lot more sheep and goats, domestic animals, than before; but the bush animals are a lot fewer.

Q: Have you noticed a lot of increase in erosion in the last number of years?

Mr. Adou: Yes, there is a lot of erosion. It can rain very heavily in a very short time. Rains used to come for a longer time and not as much in such a short time.

● ● ●

For Discussion

1. Modern agricultural technology, such as fertilizer, has clearly improved life for some Nigerians like Mr. Adou. Do you think these improvements will be lasting and sustainable?

2. How is Mr. Adou's situation like or unlike the situation that farmers in North America face?

3. What would you suggest farmers, whether in North America or Nigeria, do to avoid environmental degradation? What about urban consumers? What must they be willing to do if farmers are to make the changes you suggest?

Environmental Degradation as a Cause of Poverty

Ulf Svensson of the Swedish Foreign Ministry has noted that "just as wars lead to further degradation of the environment, an environment less able to sustain human societies as we know them today may easily lead to even more wars, in a struggle for even scarcer resources, such as uncontaminated soil and water. This is a vicious circle we cannot afford to be dragged into."

In the June 1987 *Bulletin of the Atomic Scientists,* Norman Myers, world-respected environmental consultant from Oxford, England, wrote: "National Security is no longer about fighting forces and weaponry alone. It relates increasingly to watersheds, croplands, forests, genetic resources, climate, and other factors rarely considered by military experts and political leaders."

Soil, water, forests, grasslands, and fisheries are all prime components of a nation's natural resource base. Even climatic patterns and physical-biological cycles are essential to maintain the life-support systems of a nation. If a nation's environmental foundations are disturbed or depleted, its economy may well decline, its social fabric may deteriorate, and its political structure may become destabilized.

The likely outcome is conflict, whether in the form of disorder or revolution within the nation or war with other nations. Soil erosion and agricultural decline have produced environmental refugees, fueled food riots, driven rural subsistence farmers to urban shantytowns, and even helped topple governments.

Why and how are so many nations impoverishing their people and risking their own security by destroying the environment? There are at least three causes behind this overall source of poverty.

Cause 9: Incompatibility of Today's Economic Systems with Nature's Laws

The world economic system—with North America, Europe, and Japan leading the way—is based on continuous growth in a world of finite resources. But as the world reaches nature's limits, competition for resources increases. Those in stronger positions can better compete for those resources, and so the rich tend to exploit the poor.

Clearly some areas do need economic growth. But if humankind continues its current overall trend toward growth economics, it will perpetuate poverty among the world's millions. Economic assumptions do not describe the real natural world. Examples: *continual growth and expansion; material gain is success; science can solve any problem.* There is no free lunch in nature. When scientists, technicians, and business people attempt to circumvent nature's rules, they exploit natural resources or poor people or both.

Neglect of stewardship for the earth has directly produced much of the poverty on earth today. Behind Western economic assumptions about continual growth lies a lack of any *theology of the land*—land being all the natural resources needed for human survival. As people have flocked to the cities, they have largely forgotten the importance of the land.

Rediscovering the creation story would help modern Westerners remember that the earth, the land, is a gift. Human beings were created in *the image of God* to be stewards, caretakers, trustees, managers, or co-creators with God. They were commissioned to see that the earth provides amply for the rest of God's creation. Principles such as the *Jubilee* (Leviticus 25) are now largely absent from modern thinking. Yet the earth too needs regular rest and restoration.

Cause 10: Divorce Between Urban and Rural Culture

One of the most vivid symbols of both poverty and a straining environment is the urban squalor of many third-world cities—if indeed the term *city* still applies. Modern urban centers attract the rural poor with the promise of sharing in progress. But for most, the dream of finding good regular work proves elusive, and they end up in sprawling squatter settlements on the land surrounding the cities.

In many cases, these areas are steep, dangerous, and increasingly eroded hillsides. Sanitation is poor to nonexistent. The migrants must improvise to hook up electricity and find fuel or drinking water. Though their earnings may have been meager in the countryside, they were at least productive. Now many earn equally meager incomes in nonproductive activities like peddling cigarettes, candy, or lottery tickets on the streets.

Had society valued rural culture and work enough to make land and technical assistance available to the rural poor, life in both city and countryside would be better. But instead, urban policymakers and consumers have little understanding of agriculture as a culture—a sustainable and sustaining way of life. Agriculture has become an industry and has taken on the same logic of exploitive continual-growth economics described above. Concentration of land ownership and the dominance of export crops are part of the pattern. *Agribusiness*, not *agriculture*, links urban and rural people together. Otherwise, their lives are divorced.

This divorce is just as real in North America as in the third world. Corporations control more and more land in Canada and the U.S. On the family farms that remain, many farmers have lost their sense of farming as a culture, a way of life. Like others around them, they view it as a business. Over the last generation, rather than living modestly and simply, they have sought ever-increasing profits. Farmers want to get rich like everyone else. But the kind of industrial, mechanized agriculture that now dominates North America has indebted family farmers while eroding and poisoning the land.

Back overseas, third-world governments seek to develop domestic food production for their own political security. But they have looked to Western agriculture as a model of success and want to use the latest technology. Many foreign-aid agencies lend money for such technology rather than funding policies designed to help peasants in small, less-spectacular ways. Agribusiness is eager to advise on large-scale technical agriculture—for a profit.

But the kind of large-scale energy-intensive Western agriculture that multinationals use in the third world does not really address the underlying problems of rural hunger and poverty. Worldwide many more jobs will be needed as the year 2000 approaches. A good long-term food policy will emphasize increased employment in agricultural development, education, health care, and land redistribution.[1]

Multinational agribusinesses are not prepared to do this. In fact, they do the opposite. They buy up the best land for large-scale export cropping. Their technology decreases local employment rather than creating it.

Cause 11: Regional Overpopulation

For now, most scholars do not consider the earth as a whole to be overpopulated. There is enough food for all to have an adequate diet. Fair distribution is the challenge.

But the earth *cannot* sustain present rates of growth both in consumption and population. The combination of overconsumption by the rich and regional overpopulation by the poor is one of the most serious obstacles to the elimination of poverty. Overpopulation eventually destroys the resource base in a region and leads to deeper poverty.

At the same time, poverty is the primary cause of overpopulation. As the socioeconomic status of a population increases, the birth rate decreases. Adequate food production and employment are the two most important factors in stabilizing human population.

In previous centuries, third-world populations were stable. Because the poor were particularly vulnerable, they tended to have larger families. Poor people perceive the need for many children to help in farm work and for old-age security. As science and health technology became available to underdeveloped countries, life spans increased while birth rates remained constant. The result, in the twentieth century, has been a population explosion. Competition for local food and space has led to increasing hunger and poverty. Just distribution of food produced has not kept up with the population increase.

A vicious cycle of poverty, overpopulation, hunger, and poverty has thus occurred. No sane person would devalue the health improvements that have contributed to population growth. But we want to decrease human suffering in the long run and avoid perpetuating the cycle of poverty and overpopulation. Efforts to control population growth must be part of integrated development programs. These programs include increased food production, job creation, and just distribution of the resources and opportunities needed to acquire food.

● ● ●

For Further Discussion

4. Do you expect your grandchildren, or the grandchildren of close friends, to live as well as you do? By what standards?

5. Name three or four signs of a deteriorating environment that you can observe in your area any day of the year. How do they affect you personally? Are they in some way life-threatening, or do they merely seem uncomfortable? Who might they affect more seriously—now and in coming years?

6. If you live in an urban area or are not involved in agriculture, what do you know about the people who produce your food and their struggles? If you are involved in agriculture, what would you like urban people to know?

7. Which of your current actions and choices will help future generations enjoy a reasonable quality of life? Which will make that harder?

8. Do you agree that overpopulation is as much a *result* of poverty as a *cause*? Explain.

● ● ●

Scriptures for Reflection

One reason humanity is quickly degrading the environment, and leaving poverty in the wake, is lack of a *theology of the land*. Meditate on the following Scriptures, study them in their contexts, and list some basic elements for a theology of the land: Genesis 1:20-21; 2:15; Leviticus 25:23-24; Psalm 24:1; and Romans 8:19-22.

● ● ●

Ideas for Action

1. Even if you live in the city, keep close to the culture of the land by planting and tending a garden. Use organic fertilizer; and compost table scraps, kitchen refuse, and lawn clippings. Use as few pesticides as possible and only those that are the least toxic. Share produce with friends and neighbors. Plant extra for low-income households. If you lack space outdoors, pots or containers on windowsills are just right for growing herbs and a tomato plant or two.

2. Plant trees and shrubs. Green plants use carbon dioxide, helping to decrease the greenhouse effect. In turn, they add oxygen to the atmosphere. Conifers strategically planted cut down on strong winds near homes and reduce soil erosion. Trees also provide shelter for birds and small animals. Plant trees to celebrate special occasions, such as the birth of a child, or as a memorial. Various government agencies sell tree

seedlings at low cost for replanting large areas of bare land. Reforesting such land could be a group or family project.

3. Join the glass, aluminum, paper, and plastic recyclers in your community. In the U.S., call the Environmental Protection Agency hotline (1-800-424-9346) to find out who is already doing recycling. If there is no local recycling project, begin one. Start by analyzing what your community does for waste disposal and management. Research what other communities are doing to keep their areas healthy. (See addresses below.)

Think of your volunteer recycling project as a first step toward convincing your city council or county government to endorse, plan for, adopt, and budget for official recycling programs. Design private projects for maximum effect in terms of education and advocacy.

In the meantime, recycle as a family and as a church. Reuse, recycle, make do, and avoid disposables as you follow a less consumptive lifestyle and use fewer of the earth's resources. *Alley picking* for usable items that others have thrown away can be an awareness-raising participant sport. Collect what you find at the church, sell it, and dedicate the money earned to a local justice project. The church will become an economic center while related homes clean up their act. With publicity, posters, and displays, your sale will provide a witness beyond that of traditional church rummage sales.

4. As a church, ban the use of Styrofoam cups and plates for coffee hour and potluck dinners. Explain and discuss this as a total congregation and make a policy for all groups, including renters, who use the church facilities. Donate mugs to the church as an alternative. Explain the new policy to all visitors with a prominent sign. If the congregation is skeptical, dramatize the need by rinsing and saving all Styrofoam products for a month or two, then deposit them before the altar. (Buried in landfills by the millions, Styrofoam cups nearly have eternal life!)

5. Do not tire of conserving energy. Bicycle. Support legislation to revitalize public transportation at local, state, provin-

cial, and national levels. Use it whenever and wherever possible. In smaller towns where public transportation is not economically viable, organize car pools and encourage local governments to do the same.

● ● ●

To Keep Connecting

Au Sable Institute, 7526 Sunset Trail NE, Mancelona, Mich. 49659 (616-587-8686). A Christian organization promoting environmental stewardship based on scriptural teachings. Offers courses to some eighty evangelical colleges and educational resources to denominations and individual congregations to help churches become *creation awareness centers.* Hosts annual forum on Christianity and ecology.

Concern, Inc., 1794 Colombia Road NW, Washington, D.C. 20009 (202-328-8160). Encourages citizens to get involved in decisions about waste management in their local communities. Provides resources for setting up recycling projects.

Eco-Justice Project, Anabel Taylor Hall, Cornell University, Ithaca, N.Y. 14853 (607-255-4225). Publishes *The Egg: A Journal of Eco-Justice* together with the Eco-Justice Working Group, a forum for church staff people in various denominations concerned about environmental issues.

Energy Probe Research Foundation, 100 College Street, Toronto, Ont. M5G 1L5 (416-978-7014).

Environmental Action, 1525 New Hampshire Avenue NW, Washington, D.C. 20036 (202-745-4870). National political lobbying and educational organization on issues like energy conservation, nuclear power, clean air, solid and toxic waste. Provides readable fact packets.

International Alliance for Sustainable Agriculture, 1701 University Avenue SE, Room 202, Minneapolis, Minn. 55414 (612-331-1099). Works to develop economically viable, ecologically sound, socially just, and humane agricultural systems around the world. Major program areas: research and documentation, organizational support and network building, education and public outreach.

National Recycling Coalition, 1718 M Street NW, Suite 294, Washington, D.C. 20036 (202-659-6883). Lobbying and information network on recycling. Will split the cost of sending out technical experts to help set up local recycling projects.

Rural Advancement Fund and National Sharecroppers Fund, P.O. Box 1029, Pittsboro, N.C. 27312 (919-542-5292). Works with black and white small farmers and share-croppers, helping them hold onto land and stay in farming. Stresses sustainable methods of farming. Rural Advancement Fund International, at the same address, does similar work in the third world while maintaining endangered species.

Note

1. Ronald J. Sider, *Rich Christians in an Age of Hunger: A Biblical Study* (Downers Grove, Ill.: InterVarsity Press, 1977), pp. 203-23.

15

Cycles of Poverty and Webs of Culture

SHANTI'S NAME means *peace* in Nepali. She is about twenty-seven years old and has four children. She works as a cook for North American development workers who live in this mostly Hindu nation wedged between China and India.

Shanti's husband is an alcoholic. He is around the home sometimes, but generally he is away. For several months he has been working in Pokhara, about 150 kilometers north of Butwal, where Shanti lives. He makes a good wage (about 700 to 800 rupees per month as compared to her 575 per month). The problem is that he spends most of it on alcohol.

Shanti has sent quite a few letters to find out what her husband is doing but has not received a single reply. Actually, she and her family feel that the husband's absence is basically good. As long as he's not around, they can live in peace. Before, he would come home drunk late at night and would not let them sleep.

They do miss him sometimes, because during periods of great affection, he has sometimes brought home lots of food. Everyone in Nepal prefers rice to other staples such as millet and unleavened bread. If a family eats rice and lentils regularly, the Nepalese consider them well-off. Because Shanti works for a foreigner, she is able to buy some rice herself, though at a cost of well over half her monthly salary. She has to take out loans with local shopkeepers.

Unfortunately, Shanti's family is by no means an exception. Many homes in Nepal are divided because the husbands are alcoholic.

Cultural factors are important causes of poverty. People suffer from stifling habits, exploitation, discrimination, lack of training, fatalistic attitudes, and greed. Alternative lifestyles are hard to imagine or implement.

● ● ●

For Discussion

1. Do you think Shanti should spend nearly 70 percent of her wages on rice just because it is a symbol of wealth and well-being in her culture? Think of the consumer choices you make even though they are not strictly necessary.

2. Alcoholism, drug use, and exploitive sexual relationships are prevalent, or at least more visible, among the poor. In what sense are these causes of poverty? In what sense are they symptoms of poverty?

3. A majority of the interviews and accounts of poor people in this book have been with women. A majority of poor people around the world are female. Why do you think this is so?

Cause 12: *The Legacy of Conquest, Slavery, and Colonialism*

European conquest and colonial rule exploited many peoples, keeping them powerless and poor. In some cases the conquerors deliberately destroyed the cultural wealth of native peoples as a way to control resources and prevent rebellion. In other cases, the glitter of Western consumer prosperity has lured people away from their traditional communities, clans, and lifestyles.

In North America, European settlers pushed back native peoples through violence, deception, and one-sided treaties.

Peoples and tribes who considered harmony with the earth to be their greatest wealth ended up on barren reservations far from the green lands of their forebears. They remain the poorest minority group in both the U.S. and Canada. European traders and North American settlers also brought Africans to the U.S. against their will. Emancipation of slaves during the U.S. Civil War alone could not undo the damage done to people long treated as property and fragmented whenever slave owners chose to sell that "property," splitting up families. Then, when U.S. society offered other groups an invitation to the "American dream," it long presented Afro-Americans with "Whites Only" signs.

In Latin America, conquest and enslavement were a single act. Most Spaniards and Portuguese first went, not to settle, but to pilfer gold and silver and return home rich. When they discovered that precious metals did not pave streets in the New World, they began to extract it from mines instead. For that, they needed plentiful manual labor; so they enslaved indigenous peoples in many parts of the Americas. Millions died of inhuman labor, malnutrition, and European illnesses. Where indigenous groups survived, their cultures are often but a shell of earlier glory. And when Europeans did stay and settle, the agricultural system they created was essentially feudalistic. The pattern survives in much of Latin America to this day.

In Africa, in the nineteenth century, European nations competed with each other to snatch up colonies, control empires, and insure continuing supplies of raw materials, national prestige, and geopolitical power. The European powers eventually brokered their competition with treaties that reflected little knowledge of African geography and peoplehood. The colonies they created gained independence in the mid-twentieth century, but borders drawn back in Europe remain. Few African nations are natural economic or ethnic units. New leaders have had to contend with handicapped economies and contentious tribal divisions. In addition to unnatural borders, governmental structures inherited from the colonial era are often barely viable or in touch with local reality.

Asia fared somewhat better, since the West tended to go there more in search of trade than for territory. In the name of free trade, however, Western powers imposed unequal treaties and sold unwanted products, including opium. In China, this contributed to the disintegration of an ancient civilization and to a century of political upheaval. In the Philippines and Southeast Asia, colonial patterns followed those in Latin America and Africa.

Today the colonial legacy continues, though in somewhat different forms. According to the international division of labor, developing nations are expected to provide raw materials, while industrialized nations provide finished goods. The economic theory of comparative advantage promises that developing and industrial nations will both fare better if they specialize.

But in practice, control of markets, credit, and prices for raw materials gravitates to the banks, governments, industries, and corporations centered in the developed world. Producers of raw materials are often entirely vulnerable.

Furthermore, the transnational corporations that carry out much of the actual exchange of goods and services commonly find ways to skirt the control of all governments. They have taken the role of colonial governments in keeping people poor by monopolizing prime agricultural land and mineral resources, making local people dependent on their products and employment. Large industries dominate many North American communities in similar ways, by controlling all the land or other resources. The coal mining industry in Appalachia is a classic example.

Cause 13: Racial Discrimination

Behind the history of conquest, slavery, and colonialism, but also outliving it, is racial discrimination. For one group of people to dominate others—whether white European colonialists sailing the world, a ruling tribe in Africa, or the Brahman caste in traditional India—it needs a sense of its own superiority and others' inferiority. Dominant groups often claim the support of some divine mandate to rule. Occasionally, the responsibility to "uplift" lesser races and nations is part of the theory, but never to the point that others might challenge their domineering power. Thus Rudyard Kipling wrote a poem on "The White Man's Burden."

Neglecting fellow human beings and underrating their suffering also come more easily if we see poverty as somehow normal for the people of another race. Public concern for the homeless in North America has been revealing in this respect. Not until news media began to tell the stories of once-middle-class white people suddenly out of work and out-of-doors did most North Americans take note.

Segregation in North America is illegal, but the white majority has quickly tired of correcting the damage segregationist policies have caused. Racial minorities are still the *last to be hired and the first to be fired.* Racism, then, does not need caste systems, apartheid, or segregationist laws to make and keep people poor.

Cause 14: Discrimination Against Women

Women and children bear the brunt of poverty throughout the world. Pay is universally lower for women, and work that women do outside the money economy often does not count as work at all. Custom and law hem women in. Education and training go first to men. Men are far more likely than women to abandon their children, leaving women struggling to hold families together as men go on to other pleasures.

In 1986, the U.S. conference of Roman Catholic bishops wrote a pastoral letter on economics. It noted that U.S. economic and family life undermined rather than supported each other. "Destructive trends of breakdown of traditional family life are present in all sectors of society," but "for the poor they tend to be more visible."

Alimony payments provide one example. Although men of all classes are sometimes delinquent in supporting their children after a divorce, the effects of marital breakup get worse as one moves farther down the income scale. Divorced, once-middle-class women are the fastest growing segment of the "new poor" in North America. Forty percent of white female-headed households are poor; 60 percent of black female-headed households are poor. Alone in child care and stuck in service sector jobs, they work at low pay, part-time, or not at all.

Throughout the world, even where families and marriages remain intact, modern Western economies have meant changes in the division of labor between men and women. In turn, the value placed on the work of women has changed. In self-supporting agricultural economies, men and women make different but equally important contributions to what is a single productive unit. But the more people work for money, the less society values work that does not earn money or produce saleable goods. Men often don't consider "women's work" as work at all. Since men think they are doing the "real work," they expect more and better food when it may be scarce.

Simply increasing the income or production of men does not always help, or trickle down to, women and children. Studies in various continents and many cultures consistently show that if a man receives more resources, he will spend a larger portion on nonessentials—consumer items, alcohol, other women. But increase the income of women, and they will invest it in the family, not only for more and better food but also for education.

Actually, women do more agricultural work in the world than Western development workers first assumed. Unfortunately, training in third-world agriculture happened between male development workers and local men. Yet in Africa, women do 60 to 80 percent of the agriculture work.

Cause 15: Lack of Appropriate Education and Training

In the cycle of poverty, lack of appropriate education and training is often the connecting link that closes the vicious circle and bars escape. Worldwide, literacy rates vary from 8 percent in Somalia to 100 percent in Norway and 99 percent in Barbados, Canada, Switzerland, U.S., U.S.S.R., and certain other countries. These vast inequities in education help keep poor people poor and rich people rich. A report from Africa says that a farmer with a fourth-grade education realizes a 13 percent higher crop yield than her neighbor with no education. Only half the school-age population is in school in the developing world. In Burkino Faso, the number is only 8 percent; in Niger, 15 percent.[1]

Just as serious as the lack of any education, however, is the lack of *appropriate* education. Those who are in school in developing countries often receive schooling that has little to do with the real-life skills they need. Filipinos still joke about how under U.S. colonial rule in the early twentieth century, U.S. textbooks and teachers taught them that *A* is for apple— something they had never seen. Today, *A* is for avocado.

Many former colonies inherited British, French, or Dutch school systems and still use textbooks and curricula that emphasize rote learning. The facts students memorize in India or Jamaica might have some value in Great Britain but nothing to do with their own communities. What they actually "learn" is that only modern, Western, urban culture is valuable. The message is that to improve their lot or live an interesting life, they need to move out of their traditional, "backward" communities.

The result is a massive, worldwide brain drain from countryside to city, and from third world to first world. But seldom are there enough jobs in the city to fulfill the promise that a degree will automatically mean a better life. And only rarely do better-educated doctors and teachers choose to take their skills back to the countryside.

Cause 16: Traditional Acceptance of Poverty

Conquest and domination by another race or nation can leave cultural traces for generations to come. When others always seem to have the organizational power and technological know-how, people will start to belittle their own abilities.

Fatalism results, reinforcing the cycle of poverty.

But both rich and poor are guilty of fatalism, the belief that "what has been done will be done again; there is nothing new under the sun." But Ecclesiastes 1:9 presents that idea as faulty human wisdom, not God's. No one who believes it will work to change either their own situation or society.

A mother in Bolivia looks at her sick child and says, "If God wills that he die, he will die. This is the destiny of the *campesino,* to suffer and to die." "If God wills" is a common expression on many continents, but often it has more to do with resignation than with faith. "We're a hopeless mess," say some Bolivians, but "that's life."

Such expressions are frustrating to development workers and social activists who expect the poor to take risks for the sake of change. But for those who are poor and have seen little change, except for the worse, fatalism may seem to be a safe and sensible way to understand the world. It is the fatalism of those who have the power to change that is really destructive.

The rich may be "movers and shakers" when it comes to improving their own lot. But propose measures promoting a more just society, and they protest: "You just can't engineer social justice or legislate morality."

And whenever the nonpoor despair that they, their families, or their churches can make a difference in the face of humanity's massive problems, that too is fatalism. Church people are fond of using the Scripture "The poor you will always have with you" (Matthew 26:6-13; Mark 14:3-9; John 12:1-8) to justify the presence of poor people among us. But this was an observation by Jesus, not a command. The Old Testament text he was quoting goes on to urge persistence in aiding the poor, not surrender (see Deuteronomy 15:11).

Cause 17: Human Selfishness, Greed—and Sin

Even if it were possible to counter all the causes of poverty, sin would remain. To overcome their selfishness, both the rich and the poor need transformation through the new life that is possible in the person, message, life, death, and resurrection of Jesus Christ. Without that, humanity will merely accomplish what one might call a rearranging of the furnishings. An old quip about the difference between capitalism and socialism says it: "Under capitalism, man exploits man. Under socialism, it's just the reverse."

Selfish desires and wrong motives trigger fights and quarrels. James 4:1-3 goes to the heart of all causes of poverty and injustice: "What causes fights and quarrels among you? Don't they come from your desires that battle within you? You want something but don't get it. You kill and covet, but you cannot have what you want. You quarrel and fight. You do not have, because you do not ask God. When you ask, you do not receive, because you ask with wrong motives, that you may spend what you get on your pleasures."

James 5:1-6 is even harder on the rich with regard to injustice. But the nonpoor see the poor spending what little they have on fleeting pleasures. They feel justified in asking whether the poor would do any better if society suddenly turned the tables and rich and poor exchanged places. The poor waste resources on alcohol, drugs, illicit sex, fast cars, or expensive tastes in food (Shanti's rice). Poor men exploit poor women and abandon their own children.

Christians are well-placed to see through to the sinful heart of human poverty and to offer the gospel of Jesus Christ as a solution. But since that is so, they must strive to understand how sin actually works in the world. Okay, *Jesus is the answer*; but what is the question?

Sin, it turns out, is not simply an individual reality. All the causes of poverty we have listed, not only in this chapter but in others as well, describe what the Bible means by *principalities* and *powers*. Sin weaves itself intimately into cultures, institutions, economic systems, and political programs. There seems to be no way to remove injustice without reducing society to a chaotic pile of threads. That is why the gospel of Jesus Christ is the good news of God's kingdom—a dramatically new social reality where people, both in their personal lives and together, do God's will "on earth as it is in heaven."

And that is why it is impossible to deal with other people's sin without first dealing with our own, both personally and collectively. We cannot remove the speck in another's eye without first removing the plank in our own (Matthew 7:1-5). We cannot repent of other people's sins—neither vices of the poor nor injustices of the rich. But our own repentance can begin to undo the "sins of the fathers" passed down through history. Our task is to repent of our own materialism, love of comfort, and greed, as these sins express themselves both personally and collectively.

What we *can* do for one another is help weave the just fabric of new communities—the new circles of rich, poor, and nonpoor that we discovered in part one of this book. We need God, and we need God's work through our neighbors and our others. As pervasive as sin may be, as prone as the human spirit is toward greed and envy, James promises that God gives us "more grace" (KJV) even than that. Grace does not come through quarreling over the blame for sin that we all share. "That is why Scripture says: 'God opposes the proud but gives grace to the humble' "(James 4:6).

• • •

For Further Discussion

4. List expressions of fatalism that you have heard. Name times you have despaired that society or the world could be any more just or humane toward the poor than it is. What gives you hope that change is possible?

5. If a community suddenly loses a major industry and unemployment rises, the incidence of alcoholism and domestic violence (spouse and child abuse) will soon begin to rise. Who is responsible? What should be done?

6. How can Christians repent of the collective sin of the society, economic class, or nation in which they live?

• • •

Scriptures for Reflection

Study and discuss the following texts: Revelation 18:9-13; Galatians 3:26-29; Ephesians 1:19-21; 2:10; Proverbs 30:7-9.

• • •

Ideas for Action

1. Plan a cultural fair in your community. Invite people from many backgrounds and make sure that everyone takes part in the planning from the start. The fair could involve art, music, and sciences. Each cultural community might develop displays on their experiences and understandings of peacemaking. Or the fair's theme might be a social justice agenda affecting the whole community—affordable housing, unemployment, racism, or cultural tolerance. There could be great healing power in people coming together publicly to address such an issue.

2. Organize a congregational exchange with a faith community of a different cultural heritage. Arrange to spend a long weekend with the people of another congregation. Learn about worship styles, ways of being together, playing and sharing, or even ways of resolving conflict. Make sure that each group is able to get a feel for the experience of the other.

3. Host workshops on racism and cultural awareness in your congregation or your community. For models of how to put together a sensitization workshop, write to the General Commission on Religion and Race, United Methodist Church, 110 Maryland Avenue NE, No. 48, Washington, D.C. 20002 (202-547-2271). A study guide on white racism entitled *America's Original Sin* is available from *Sojourners* magazine, Box 29272, Washington, D.C. 20017 (202-636-3637). For models on how to respond to a situation in which hate groups are openly active, contact the Center for Democratic Renewal, Box 10500, Atlanta, Ga. 30310 (404-221-0025).

4. Refugees and immigrants are enriching our own cultures in North America. Welcome this gift by sponsoring a refugee family. Many denominations have programs to arrange

sponsorships and help both host congregations and refugees through their period of transition. Contact your denominational offices.

5. Develop a prayer-and-action group in your church to study how different peoples are portrayed in its curricula. They also might evaluate the materials in your church or community library.

6. Your church choir can learn more songs from other countries. For example, *Freedom Is Coming*, published in tape and songbook forms by Fortress Press, features African freedom songs. Choir and congregation can learn the Afro-American national anthem "Lift Every Voice and Sing."

● ● ●

To Keep Connecting

Children's Defense Fund, 122 C Street NW, Washington, D.C. 20001 (202-628-8787). Provides documentation on the extent and character of children in poverty in the U.S. Advocates policies promoting their welfare.

Church Women United, 475 Riverside Drive, Room 812, New York, N.Y. 10115 (212-870-2347). National movement working with over 1,500 local groups. Major emphasis is countering *the pauperization of women* through skills training and follow-up. Works closely with the Religious Network for Equality for Women (RNEW) at the same address (212-870-2995). RNEW works on legislative issues and offers a six-session study on economics for women called *Learning Economics: Empowering Women for Action.*

Farm Labor Organizing Committee, 714 South St. Clair, Toledo, Ohio 43609 (419-243-3456). Advocate for migrant farm workers. Has also worked to mediate between seasonal workers, producers, and companies.

National Association for the Advancement of Colored People (NAACP), 4805 Mt. Hope Drive, Baltimore, Md. 21215-3297 (301-358-8900). Interracial organization that has worked to end racial discrimination since 1910. Has

2,200 local chapters with half a million members.

The Overground Railroad, 722 Monroe Street, Evanston, Ill. 60202 (312-328-0772). Works on refugee issues and offers services to people who are adjusting to new cultural settings.

United Farm Workers of America, P.O. Box 62, Keene, Calif. 93531 (805-822-5571). First labor union able to organize farm workers in the U.S. Advocate for the Latino community and women. Publishes *Food and Justice* magazine. Strong commitment to active nonviolence.

United Nations Development Fund for Women, 304 East 45th Street, New York, N.Y. 10017 (212-906-5000). Since 1976 has funded 400 projects targeted to poorest women in some 100 of the world's least developed countries—technical assistance, food cycle projects, credit.

Women for Economic Justice, 145 Tremont Street, Room 607, Boston, Mass. 02111 (617-426-9734). Multicultural women's organization seeking economic equality, particularly for women of color. Most work is in Massachusetts, but provides technical assistance to groups in other states wanting to set up efforts similar to its own *Up and Out of Poverty Campaign.*

Note

1. *The World Almanac and Book of Facts 1989,* ed. by Mark S. Hoffman (New York: Pharos Books, 1988), pp. 649-737; cf. Ruth Leger Sivard, *World Military and Social Expenditures, 1987-88* (Washington, D.C.: World Priorities, 1987).

Arranging Encounters Between Middle- and Low-Income Groups[1]

Marvin Friedman Hamm

ENCOUNTERS between middle- and low-income people can take different forms. One option is to invite low-income people to come and speak with a middle-income group about their experiences of being poor. Another is for the middle-income group to go to the low-income community and encounter the life and people of that community. Going into a low-income community can be threatening. But the possibility of significant learning is much greater when participants step out of their familiar surroundings into a strange world.

Any structured meeting between middle-income people and poor people—in either setting—will require great sensitivity. Let the middle-income be on guard not to use and alienate the poor in their attempt to learn about them. In arranging the encounter, planners must take care to protect the dignity of the low-income people they are meeting. A visit to a low-income community by middle-income people can easily become a tourist excursion. The poor are not oddities to be examined or objects to be used for other people's ends—even for the transformation of the nonpoor.

Preparing for Encounter

A respectful encounter requires the informed consent of all participants. The low-income participants must know what the middle-income persons want from them and why. They must agree to be part of the learning process. The encounter must always take place in a situation of trust.

It is essential that the middle-income group have the sponsorship of a person whom the low-income community respects and trusts. This bridge-builder can be from either group. The crucial thing is that this person have the trust of both groups. Then she or he can bring the two groups together in much the same way as a person introduces two of her friends to each other. The two friends, who have not met before, already have a connection to each other through their mutual friend. When both groups trust the person who brings them together, they can come together with an openness toward each other.

If you don't already know a person who can serve as your sponsor, find one. Begin by contacting leaders in inner-city congregations or people in church-related agencies that deal with poverty and justice concerns. Or you might find social workers or other service providers in your own congregation who can serve as the bridge-builder or who can introduce you to an appropriate contact person.

In some cities there are organizations that have special inner-city exposure programs designed to help middle-income groups encounter the world of people who are poor. These organizations have already done the groundwork of arranging encounters and can be most helpful to you.

As you approach inner-city churches and agencies, you will discover a range of philosophies and styles of relating to poor people. Take care to find groups whose philosophy is compatible with your educational goals. Avoid organizations that are paternalistic and agencies that aim their programs only toward fitting people into the societal status quo. Instead, seek organizations that have a more critical evaluation of present societal structures and whose focus is working with and advocating for poor people.

Once the bridge-builder establishes that both groups are open to a meeting, he or she must prepare all the participants for the meeting. The low-income people must know something about the middle-income people they will be meeting and what kinds of questions might arise from them. Middle-income participants will need coaching on appropriate behavior. They must know that they are going into the meeting as guests and that their role is to listen and to learn. Under no circumstances are they to begin to offer advice on how low-income people should solve their problems. Nor are they to ask prying questions or barge into sensitive and difficult topics. They are to listen with empathy. There may be room for asking questions, but only with respect and sensitivity.

As part of their preparation for the encounter, the middle-income participants should have an opportunity to set goals for their time together. The leaders of the program will have set the basic purpose and focus of the program, but they should invite participants to set personal goals. This will give them a greater sense of ownership in the learning process.

Structuring Encounter

Only the resources and time available to the group will limit the creative possibilities of the encounter. Based on my experience with several existing programs, I offer the following suggestions for structuring the encounter.

Hearing stories. One powerful way of encountering the experience of poverty is to listen to poor people's stories and experiences. This may mean having people tell their stories. Or it may mean asking a group of people to talk about their experiences with a particular institution, such as the welfare system, schools, public housing, or employers.

Two things are important: One, the middle-income people should hear the facts—how people are exploited, neglected, abandoned; how they have struggled; their failures and successes. Two, the middle-income people should taste the feelings behind the stories—the pain, the despair, the hope. Hearing stories can be a holy time. Stories have a way of slipping through all our rationalizations and preconceptions. They have a way of touching us at the core of our beings.

In a meeting for storytelling, poor people become the teachers, guides, and experts. They know the territory and open themselves to share their knowledge and experience with their guests. As they teach and guide middle-income people, they can gather a sense of empowerment.

Entering the reality of the poor. In this type of encounter, middle-income people enter into part of the experience of poor people. For example, the group might split up and visit the homes of poor families and, if possible, live with them for a weekend or longer. (This would require an especially high level of trust by all the participants in the bridge-builder and some careful preparation). Participants might sit in a welfare office to see the treatment of clients and to experience the waiting.

Another more difficult form of entering into the experience of poverty is the *urban plunge.* Here participants receive a few dollars, are dropped off in the inner city (usually in groups of two or three), and must fend for themselves for a few days. They become homeless people and have to find their own shelter, food, and security.

A modified form of the urban plunge is for groups of middle-income people to go on one-day excursions into the city streets. They might wait in temporary labor pool waiting rooms, eat in soup kitchens, hang out in parks and on street corners, and search in abandoned buildings and underneath bridges for the *homes* of homeless people. These kinds of experiences allow middle-income people to begin to know how poor people live. Then they can feel difficulties and horrors that poor people face every day. Again, poor people can serve as the guides and interpreters for these experiences.

Sharing activities. The intent of shared activities between middle-income and poor people is to break down barriers of unfamiliarity and alienation between the two groups. It is to help each group recognize their common humanity and build relationships. Shared activities, shared rituals, and shared experience help make connections with people in ways that more formal programs and encounters cannot. Possible activities are shared meals, informal social times, shared worship, and working together on a common task or project (maybe a neighborhood cleanup day or a building project).

Learning Together

When we bring people into situations that lead them to doubt their understandings of the world, their values, and even their life choices, we must proceed with care. To suddenly realize that I am living comfortably while others are suffering deeply, to recognize the distorted ways I see my world, can be very threatening. My basic self-identity and worldview can begin to unravel.

Leaders who provoke this process must be careful not to push people too hard. They also should avoid evoking feelings that are deeper than can be adequately processed in the time available. The temptation might be to shock or stun the participants, in the hope that this will lead to their eventual transformation. To do so is irresponsible and may do more harm than good. It can lead people to cynicism or block out all further questioning. There must be a delicate balance between tearing down and building up, between holding people on the edge and supporting them. It is important to realize the limitations of time and to structure the program accordingly.

It is also crucial that participants have opportunity to express and process their feelings. Otherwise, they may be unable to move beyond them toward transformation. Encounters with people who are poor can trigger powerful emotions in middle-income participants. Participants might feel shock and horror at what they see. They may want to help, to make things better. Yet they may feel overwhelmed and helpless. They may feel guilty for their comfortable lives.

To be in someone else's world, where they don't know how to act appropriately, might feel strange and threatening. Hearing and seeing the anguish of others may put them in touch with their own suppressed anguish. They may feel disoriented. Many will attempt to repress and deny feelings and thoughts that threaten to disrupt their way of seeing and being in the world.

The leaders must work with the group to create a supportive and open climate, where participants can feel free to name and own their disquieting feelings. There is no room here for judging or denying the validity of these feelings or for doing anything that promotes paralyzing guilt. The leaders and the group must proceed delicately, with gentleness. Middle-income participants may need to withdraw from their encounter with the poor for a while to process the experience in a place where they feel safe, comfortable, and uninhibited.

By encountering poor people as people and immersing themselves in the reality of poverty, participants will probably begin rethinking their assumptions about poverty. Stories of the public school system's neglect of poor children immediately reveal how that institution pushes people toward the margins of society. A visit to a temporary labor agency brings participants face-to-face with economic exploitation.

Most participants will quickly recognize that *blaming the victim* does not adequately account for these realities. They will begin an internal search for a new framework by which to make sense of what they see. It is important to allow participants to express this internal search and to bring it into the group dialogue.

If resources and time allow, one might introduce alternative ways for interpreting poverty and discussing whether they apply to the situation at hand. For example, a group concerned about homelessness could begin by meeting with a group of homeless people. The homeless people could tell of the events that brought them to living on the streets and talk about the obstacles they face in getting off the streets.

Then, with the homeless people present, the leaders could present statistics on the depletion of low-income housing and on the rise of a permanent underclass of unemployed people. This information could be supplemented by an account of how companies increasingly operate globally rather than nationally, and what this means for jobs and markets. The entire group could discuss these interpretative models in the light of the experiences of the homeless people, to see whether they fit.

There are some hazards in presenting *intellectual* models for understanding poverty. Moving into *rational* analysis can give participants a route of escape from God's call for compassion to the poor. The introduction of *expert* interpretations can short-circuit the group's dialogue and turn the group away from naming its own reality. If group leaders or others offer alternative frames of interpretation, they must be sure to encourage the group to dialogue with these models.

Processing an Encounter

Either toward the end of an encounter, or soon afterward, participants should be able to reflect on what has happened to them. How have they reacted and why? If they can discover the answers to these questions for themselves, they will move a long way toward recognizing the beliefs that have shaped their attitudes toward people who are poor. If they can evaluate their previous outlook in light of the biblical tradition, they may sense a call to change both their beliefs and their actions.

I see four distinct steps in this process:

Sharing feelings. Group leaders ask participants to share their reactions, especially their feelings. Some of these will have already emerged spontaneously during the experience, but it is important that the group again make them present. In relation to each part of the encounter, leaders can ask questions aimed at naming feelings: What struck you about. . .? How did you feel when. . .? The leaders should proceed with gentleness, being supportive of all feelings that emerge, not negating them in any way.

Leaders should be especially attentive to strong feelings of compassion or powerful anger against the institutions that oppress poor people. Also listen for feelings that distance the participants from the pain they have encountered or reactions that deny disconcerting aspects of the experience. For example, participants may be angry at those who presented alternative social analysis. Watch for tendencies to intellectualize the experience, to talk about how someone else should respond, to debate the issue abstractly, or to jump to superficial interpretations and proposals for response. Each of these responses can be a flight from the encounter with suffering and the call to compassion. Listen closely for signs of disorientation—for example, fears about what this means for participants' lives or guilt about all the material goods and opportunities they enjoy.

Exploring value systems. Begin to explore the basis of these feelings, especially defensive and disoriented feelings. The intent here is for participants to name and explore the values by which they shape their lives—the belief system that their defensive feelings are protecting but which the experience has breached. Now it is time for participants to go back and look at why they reacted as they did.

The facilitator might invite the participants to reflect on what it is about their present way of seeing and relating to poor people that they are defensive or disoriented about. Then there should be an opportunity to critically evaluate these perspectives and actions.

Leaders might ask participants why they feel angry about a new model of social analysis. This is an invitation to articulate their own interpretations of poverty. Then leaders might ask the group to reflect on where their interpretations came from, where or how they learned them. Participants should also have the chance to say why they feel afraid of what their new awareness of poverty might mean for their lives. What is being threatened? What values and actions are being questioned?

Hearing the Bible. The participants bring their perspectives into dialogue with the biblical tradition. They now examine their own lives in light of their encounter with the poor and in the light of the biblical call for compassion and justice.

Converting to the poor. The facilitator invites participants to choose new values and actions. They must act on new insights and learning gained in the encounter and evaluation if change is to be real and lasting. Learning is as much in the doing as it is in thinking. The values and perspectives of a person who serves poor people, and who lives and acts in solidarity with them, come as the person begins to live in this new way. Deep conversion to the poor happens within an acting and reflecting community concerned for justice. Conversion from self-centeredness to love emerges in community and relationship with people who are poor.

From Encounter to Commitment

This process begins in a short-term immersion program and extends far beyond it. But the conversion can begin as participants evaluate their encounter with the poor. At the end of the encounter and reflection, it is important to give the group an opportunity to identify their learning and to make choices about next steps they might want to take.

To help the group identify learnings, go back to the objectives that participants set for themselves at the outset of the program. In the group, people can evaluate whether they reached their objectives and specify what they gained. The leaders might facilitate this by asking: What did you learn about poor people? What new insights did you gain into the way society works? What did you learn about yourself, your attitudes? What insights will you take with you?

Key questions: What are the things that moved you deeply? What were the things that stirred your heart? To what situations did you feel an inner compulsion to respond? Did anyone's story and example especially touch you? Such queries invite the participants to become conscious of any *callings* that have come to them during the time together. These become special openings to their movement out of old patterns to new actions and new understandings.

After the participants have carefully reflected on their learning and insights, the leaders can encourage them to make commitments to follow up on them. They may invite individuals, and the group as a whole, to identify what they want to do with the insights. It is important here that the participants not speak about what others should do, but about what they—personally and corporately—want to do.

Leaders can ask: Are there more things that you would like to learn about poverty? How could you learn these? Are there personal actions that you would like to undertake in response to your learning? At this stage, the leaders could introduce some volunteer opportunities for participants. The leaders can ask if the group would like to continue meeting, what things they would like to learn next, and if there are any responses they want to consider together. Be concrete. Respond to any interest by setting a time and place to continue.

It is not the goal of the encounter to push participants into decisions they are not ready to make. The leaders must be careful not to manipulate. Instead, the goal is to create a space for participants to name their learning, to recognize the stirring of the Spirit within them. Then the leaders can help them recognize and choose follow-up actions by which to express their new understandings with integrity and through which they can discover a deeper conversion, a new belief system, a new self-identity, and new action for liberation.

The goals of conversion are also the means of conversion. We are converted to people who are poor as we begin to take specific—even if tentative—actions of solidarity. As we reflect on these actions in prayer and in Bible study. And as we submerge our insights into renewed actions of solidarity and liberation.

Note

1. This material on arranging encounters is adapted from Marvin Friedman Hamm, "Conversion to the Poor: Calling Middle Class Christians into Solidarity with the Urban Poor," M.A. Peace Studies thesis, Associated Mennonite Biblical Seminaries, 1988, and used with his permission. Hamm lives in Winnipeg, Manitoba. He is coordinator of a free-meal program and also works with Urban Plunge, a group that organizes inner-city encounters for church groups in Winnipeg.

Questionnaire: Beginning Social Analysis[1]

Joe Holland and Peter Henriot

BEGINNING social analysis in a local situation can be simple. First, we must ask ourselves what we know about the various sectors of our local community. What we already know—and what we don't know—will push us to further study. Below are several questions that may help us to determine the areas upon which to focus our attention.

Social

1. What is the *demographic* character of the locality?
   present population
   growth rate (decline, increase)
   projections toward the year 2000
   present geographic concentration
   projected shifts in concentration
2. What is the *racial-ethnic* situation?
   European ethnic groups
   Hispanics, including recent Central American immigrants
   African-Americans
   Native peoples
   Asian immigrants
   Other

3. What is the *cultural* character of the locality?
   ethnic heritages of population
   character, or *stamp,* of the people
   level of education
   strength of community ties
   state of the arts

4. What is the *class structure* in the locality?
   nonworking poor (or *underclass*)
   low-income service workers
   blue-collar workers
   white-collar workers
   executive class
   super rich

5. Identify the dominant *social problems* in the area related to:

abortion	migratory labor
aging	race
alcohol, drugs	schools
crime	women
families	youth
health care	other
leisure activities	

6. What is the *social-psychological temper* of the area?
   predominant values
   class divisions and conflicts
   general outlook on life: satisfaction, malaise

Economic

7. What is the general economic *profile* of the locality?
   major industries
   agricultural situation
   natural resources
   new technologies
   relationship to military industries
   role of business and labor groups in community

8. What is the economic *situation*?
   self-reliance versus dependency
   growth rate

inflation, cost of living
unemployment
income distribution
strength of unions
labor-management relations
9. What is the *environmental* situation?
pollution (air, water, land)
energy prospects, present and future
effectiveness of environmental regulations
10. What are the key economic *problems*?
renewal of capital from community versus capital flight
urban gentrification and displacement
housing
tax bases
public services
other
11. What is the relationship between the *local* economy and the *international* economy?
imports, or exports
offices of multinational corporations
foreign-owned local businesses
relocation of local industries

Political

12. What is the political *profile* of the locality?
relationship of political parties
existence of party *machines*
dominant political party
internal divisions within parties
voting registration-election turnout
church-state relationship
13. What is the nature of its political *leadership*?
record of legislators representing the area in
Parliament or Congress
record of provincial or state politicians
record of municipal or city officials
14. What is the nature of its *informal* leadership?

names of influential people
socioeconomic background of leaders
connections (business, family, etc.) with other
    influential groups or individuals
nature of power concentration
active interest groups or lobbies
15. What *nonpolitical* factors influence political life?
    churches and synagogues
    media
    business groups
    labor unions

Ecclesial

16. What is the *religious climate* in the locality?
    percentages of Catholics, Protestants, Jews, etc.
    percentage of nonreligiously affiliated
    presence of non-Judeo-Christian religions, traditions,
        or movements
    degree of ecumenical cooperation
    religious affection, disaffection (provide reasons)
17. What is the health of the *local church*?
    state of local congregations
    character of church leadership
    pastoral councils
    participation of laity
    morale, style of clergy and religious professionals
    state of church-sponsored service projects
    institutions (hospitals, schools, etc.)

Note

1. Adapted from the appendix of *Social Analysis: Linking Faith and Justice*, by Joe Holland and Peter Henriot, S.J., revised and enlarged edition (Maryknoll, N.Y.: Orbis Books, 1980 and 1983), pp. 106-109. Used with permission. Permission is hereby granted by Orbis Books to duplicate this questionnaire for local study group use.
Suggestions for using this questionnaire appear on page 88.

The Author

GERALD W. Schlabach has worked as a writer and program administrator with Mennonite Central Committee (MCC), the relief and development arm of North American Mennonite churches, since 1980. Much of that time was spent in Central America.

From 1983 through 1985, Gerald and his wife, Joetta Handrich, served as MCC country representatives in Nicaragua. While there, Gerald began developing a regional *peace portfolio* for MCC. In 1986 he relocated in Honduras and that assignment became his full-time assignment.

Gerald promoted theological education and practical training related to peace and justice issues with Central American church leaders. He has written various articles on the challenges Central America presents to historical peace churches in North America. In August 1987, he and his family returned to the United States, where he continued writing part-time for MCC while homemaking.

Gerald graduated from Goshen (Ind.) College in 1979 with a degree in history and journalism. He has attended the Associated Mennonite Biblical Seminaries in Elkhart, Indiana, and in 1989 returned there for further study.

Gerald and Joetta are members of the Michigan State University Mennonite Fellowship. They have two sons, Gabriel and Jacob.